FREE Study Skills Videos/DVD Offer

Dear Customer,

Thank you for your purchase from Mometrix! We consider it an honor and a privilege that you have purchased our product and we want to ensure your satisfaction.

As part of our ongoing effort to meet the needs of test takers, we have developed a set of Study Skills Videos that we would like to give you for FREE. These videos cover our *best practices* for getting ready for your exam, from how to use our study materials to how to best prepare for the day of the test.

All that we ask is that you email us with feedback that would describe your experience so far with our product. Good, bad, or indifferent, we want to know what you think!

To get your FREE Study Skills Videos, you can use the **QR code** below, or send us an **email** at studyvideos@mometrix.com with *FREE VIDEOS* in the subject line and the following information in the body of the email:

- The name of the product you purchased.
- Your product rating on a scale of 1-5, with 5 being the highest rating.
- Your feedback. It can be long, short, or anything in between. We just want to know your impressions and experience so far with our product. (Good feedback might include how our study material met your needs and ways we might be able to make it even better. You could highlight features that you found helpful or features that you think we should add.)

If you have any questions or concerns, please don't hesitate to contact me directly.

Thanks again!

Sincerely,

Jay Willis
Vice President
jay.willis@mometrix.com
1-800-673-8175

Series 65

Exam Secrets Study Guide

Series 65 Test Review for the Uniform Investment Adviser Law Examination

Written and edited by Mometrix Test Prep

Printed in the United States of America

This paper meets the requirements of ANSI/NISO Z39.48-1992 (Permanence of Paper).

Paperback
ISBN 13: 978-1-61072-861-4
ISBN 10: 1-6107-2861-0

Ebook
ISBN 13: 978-1-62120-457-2
ISBN 10: 1-6212-0457-X

Dear Future Exam Success Story

First of all, **THANK YOU** for purchasing Mometrix study materials!

Second, congratulations! You are one of the few determined test-takers who are committed to doing whatever it takes to excel on your exam. **You have come to the right place.** We developed these study materials with one goal in mind: to deliver you the information you need in a format that's concise and easy to use.

In addition to optimizing your guide for the content of the test, we've outlined our recommended steps for breaking down the preparation process into small, attainable goals so you can make sure you stay on track.

We've also analyzed the entire test-taking process, identifying the most common pitfalls and showing how you can overcome them and be ready for any curveball the test throws you.

Standardized testing is one of the biggest obstacles on your road to success, which only increases the importance of doing well in the high-pressure, high-stakes environment of test day. Your results on this test could have a significant impact on your future, and this guide provides the information and practical advice to help you achieve your full potential on test day.

Your success is our success

We would love to hear from you! If you would like to share the story of your exam success or if you have any questions or comments in regard to our products, please contact us at **800-673-8175** or **support@mometrix.com**.

Thanks again for your business and we wish you continued success!

Sincerely,
The Mometrix Test Preparation Team

TABLE OF CONTENTS

Introduction

Thank you for purchasing this resource! You have made the choice to prepare yourself for a test that could have a huge impact on your future, and this guide is designed to help you be fully ready for test day. Obviously, it's important to have a solid understanding of the test material, but you also need to be prepared for the unique environment and stressors of the test, so that you can perform to the best of your abilities.

For this purpose, the first section that appears in this guide is the **Secret Keys**. We've devoted countless hours to meticulously researching what works and what doesn't, and we've boiled down our findings to the five most impactful steps you can take to improve your performance on the test. We start at the beginning with study planning and move through the preparation process, all the way to the testing strategies that will help you get the most out of what you know when you're finally sitting in front of the test.

We recommend that you start preparing for your test as far in advance as possible. However, if you've bought this guide as a last-minute study resource and only have a few days before your test, we recommend that you skip over the first two Secret Keys since they address a long-term study plan.

If you struggle with **test anxiety**, we strongly encourage you to check out our recommendations for how you can overcome it. Test anxiety is a formidable foe, but it can be beaten, and we want to make sure you have the tools you need to defeat it.

Secret Key #1 – Plan Big, Study Small

There's a lot riding on your performance. If you want to ace this test, you're going to need to keep your skills sharp and the material fresh in your mind. You need a plan that lets you review everything you need to know while still fitting in your schedule. We'll break this strategy down into three categories.

Information Organization

Start with the information you already have: the official test outline. From this, you can make a complete list of all the concepts you need to cover before the test. Organize these concepts into groups that can be studied together, and create a list of any related vocabulary you need to learn so you can brush up on any difficult terms. You'll want to keep this vocabulary list handy once you actually start studying since you may need to add to it along the way.

Time Management

Once you have your set of study concepts, decide how to spread them out over the time you have left before the test. Break your study plan into small, clear goals so you have a manageable task for each day and know exactly what you're doing. Then just focus on one small step at a time. When you manage your time this way, you don't need to spend hours at a time studying. Studying a small block of content for a short period each day helps you retain information better and avoid stressing over how much you have left to do. You can relax knowing that you have a plan to cover everything in time. In order for this strategy to be effective though, you have to start studying early and stick to your schedule. Avoid the exhaustion and futility that comes from last-minute cramming!

Study Environment

The environment you study in has a big impact on your learning. Studying in a coffee shop, while probably more enjoyable, is not likely to be as fruitful as studying in a quiet room. It's important to keep distractions to a minimum. You're only planning to study for a short block of time, so make the most of it. Don't pause to check your phone or get up to find a snack. It's also important to **avoid multitasking**. Research has consistently shown that multitasking will make your studying dramatically less effective. Your study area should also be comfortable and well-lit so you don't have the distraction of straining your eyes or sitting on an uncomfortable chair.

The time of day you study is also important. You want to be rested and alert. Don't wait until just before bedtime. Study when you'll be most likely to comprehend and remember. Even better, if you know what time of day your test will be, set that time aside for study. That way your brain will be used to working on that subject at that specific time and you'll have a better chance of recalling information.

Finally, it can be helpful to team up with others who are studying for the same test. Your actual studying should be done in as isolated an environment as possible, but the work of organizing the information and setting up the study plan can be divided up. In between study sessions, you can discuss with your teammates the concepts that you're all studying and quiz each other on the details. Just be sure that your teammates are as serious about the test as you are. If you find that your study time is being replaced with social time, you might need to find a new team.

Secret Key #2 – Make Your Studying Count

You're devoting a lot of time and effort to preparing for this test, so you want to be absolutely certain it will pay off. This means doing more than just reading the content and hoping you can remember it on test day. It's important to make every minute of study count. There are two main areas you can focus on to make your studying count.

Retention

It doesn't matter how much time you study if you can't remember the material. You need to make sure you are retaining the concepts. To check your retention of the information you're learning, try recalling it at later times with minimal prompting. Try carrying around flashcards and glance at one or two from time to time or ask a friend who's also studying for the test to quiz you.

To enhance your retention, look for ways to put the information into practice so that you can apply it rather than simply recalling it. If you're using the information in practical ways, it will be much easier to remember. Similarly, it helps to solidify a concept in your mind if you're not only reading it to yourself but also explaining it to someone else. Ask a friend to let you teach them about a concept you're a little shaky on (or speak aloud to an imaginary audience if necessary). As you try to summarize, define, give examples, and answer your friend's questions, you'll understand the concepts better and they will stay with you longer. Finally, step back for a big picture view and ask yourself how each piece of information fits with the whole subject. When you link the different concepts together and see them working together as a whole, it's easier to remember the individual components.

Finally, practice showing your work on any multi-step problems, even if you're just studying. Writing out each step you take to solve a problem will help solidify the process in your mind, and you'll be more likely to remember it during the test.

Modality

Modality simply refers to the means or method by which you study. Choosing a study modality that fits your own individual learning style is crucial. No two people learn best in exactly the same way, so it's important to know your strengths and use them to your advantage.

For example, if you learn best by visualization, focus on visualizing a concept in your mind and draw an image or a diagram. Try color-coding your notes, illustrating them, or creating symbols that will trigger your mind to recall a learned concept. If you learn best by hearing or discussing information, find a study partner who learns the same way or read aloud to yourself. Think about how to put the information in your own words. Imagine that you are giving a lecture on the topic and record yourself so you can listen to it later.

For any learning style, flashcards can be helpful. Organize the information so you can take advantage of spare moments to review. Underline key words or phrases. Use different colors for different categories. Mnemonic devices (such as creating a short list in which every item starts with the same letter) can also help with retention. Find what works best for you and use it to store the information in your mind most effectively and easily.

Secret Key #3 – Practice the Right Way

Your success on test day depends not only on how many hours you put into preparing, but also on whether you prepared the right way. It's good to check along the way to see if your studying is paying off. One of the most effective ways to do this is by taking practice tests to evaluate your progress. Practice tests are useful because they show exactly where you need to improve. Every time you take a practice test, pay special attention to these three groups of questions:

- The questions you got wrong
- The questions you had to guess on, even if you guessed right
- The questions you found difficult or slow to work through

This will show you exactly what your weak areas are, and where you need to devote more study time. Ask yourself why each of these questions gave you trouble. Was it because you didn't understand the material? Was it because you didn't remember the vocabulary? Do you need more repetitions on this type of question to build speed and confidence? Dig into those questions and figure out how you can strengthen your weak areas as you go back to review the material.

Additionally, many practice tests have a section explaining the answer choices. It can be tempting to read the explanation and think that you now have a good understanding of the concept. However, an explanation likely only covers part of the question's broader context. Even if the explanation makes perfect sense, **go back and investigate** every concept related to the question until you're positive you have a thorough understanding.

As you go along, keep in mind that the practice test is just that: practice. Memorizing these questions and answers will not be very helpful on the actual test because it is unlikely to have any of the same exact questions. If you only know the right answers to the sample questions, you won't be prepared for the real thing. **Study the concepts** until you understand them fully, and then you'll be able to answer any question that shows up on the test.

It's important to wait on the practice tests until you're ready. If you take a test on your first day of study, you may be overwhelmed by the amount of material covered and how much you need to learn. Work up to it gradually.

On test day, you'll need to be prepared for answering questions, managing your time, and using the test-taking strategies you've learned. It's a lot to balance, like a mental marathon that will have a big impact on your future. Like training for a marathon, you'll need to start slowly and work your way up. When test day arrives, you'll be ready.

Start with the strategies you've read in the first two Secret Keys—plan your course and study in the way that works best for you. If you have time, consider using multiple study resources to get different approaches to the same concepts. It can be helpful to see difficult concepts from more than one angle. Then find a good source for practice tests. Many times, the test website will suggest potential study resources or provide sample tests.

Practice Test Strategy

If you're able to find at least three practice tests, we recommend this strategy:

Untimed and Open-Book Practice

Take the first test with no time constraints and with your notes and study guide handy. Take your time and focus on applying the strategies you've learned.

Timed and Open-Book Practice

Take the second practice test open-book as well, but set a timer and practice pacing yourself to finish in time.

Timed and Closed-Book Practice

Take any other practice tests as if it were test day. Set a timer and put away your study materials. Sit at a table or desk in a quiet room, imagine yourself at the testing center, and answer questions as quickly and accurately as possible.

Keep repeating timed and closed-book tests on a regular basis until you run out of practice tests or it's time for the actual test. Your mind will be ready for the schedule and stress of test day, and you'll be able to focus on recalling the material you've learned.

Secret Key #4 – Pace Yourself

Once you're fully prepared for the material on the test, your biggest challenge on test day will be managing your time. Just knowing that the clock is ticking can make you panic even if you have plenty of time left. Work on pacing yourself so you can build confidence against the time constraints of the exam. Pacing is a difficult skill to master, especially in a high-pressure environment, so **practice is vital**.

Set time expectations for your pace based on how much time is available. For example, if a section has 60 questions and the time limit is 30 minutes, you know you have to average 30 seconds or less per question in order to answer them all. Although 30 seconds is the hard limit, set 25 seconds per question as your goal, so you reserve extra time to spend on harder questions. When you budget extra time for the harder questions, you no longer have any reason to stress when those questions take longer to answer.

Don't let this time expectation distract you from working through the test at a calm, steady pace, but keep it in mind so you don't spend too much time on any one question. Recognize that taking extra time on one question you don't understand may keep you from answering two that you do understand later in the test. If your time limit for a question is up and you're still not sure of the answer, mark it and move on, and come back to it later if the time and the test format allow. If the testing format doesn't allow you to return to earlier questions, just make an educated guess; then put it out of your mind and move on.

On the easier questions, be careful not to rush. It may seem wise to hurry through them so you have more time for the challenging ones, but it's not worth missing one if you know the concept and just didn't take the time to read the question fully. Work efficiently but make sure you understand the question and have looked at all of the answer choices, since more than one may seem right at first.

Even if you're paying attention to the time, you may find yourself a little behind at some point. You should speed up to get back on track, but do so wisely. Don't panic; just take a few seconds less on each question until you're caught up. Don't guess without thinking, but do look through the answer choices and eliminate any you know are wrong. If you can get down to two choices, it is often worthwhile to guess from those. Once you've chosen an answer, move on and don't dwell on any that you skipped or had to hurry through. If a question was taking too long, chances are it was one of the harder ones, so you weren't as likely to get it right anyway.

On the other hand, if you find yourself getting ahead of schedule, it may be beneficial to slow down a little. The more quickly you work, the more likely you are to make a careless mistake that will affect your score. You've budgeted time for each question, so don't be afraid to spend that time. Practice an efficient but careful pace to get the most out of the time you have.

Secret Key #5 – Have a Plan for Guessing

When you're taking the test, you may find yourself stuck on a question. Some of the answer choices seem better than others, but you don't see the one answer choice that is obviously correct. What do you do?

The scenario described above is very common, yet most test takers have not effectively prepared for it. Developing and practicing a plan for guessing may be one of the single most effective uses of your time as you get ready for the exam.

In developing your plan for guessing, there are three questions to address:

- When should you start the guessing process?
- How should you narrow down the choices?
- Which answer should you choose?

When to Start the Guessing Process

Unless your plan for guessing is to select C every time (which, despite its merits, is not what we recommend), you need to leave yourself enough time to apply your answer elimination strategies. Since you have a limited amount of time for each question, that means that if you're going to give yourself the best shot at guessing correctly, you have to decide quickly whether or not you will guess.

Of course, the best-case scenario is that you don't have to guess at all, so first, see if you can answer the question based on your knowledge of the subject and basic reasoning skills. Focus on the key words in the question and try to jog your memory of related topics. Give yourself a chance to bring the knowledge to mind, but once you realize that you don't have (or you can't access) the knowledge you need to answer the question, it's time to start the guessing process.

It's almost always better to start the guessing process too early than too late. It only takes a few seconds to remember something and answer the question from knowledge. Carefully eliminating wrong answer choices takes longer. Plus, going through the process of eliminating answer choices can actually help jog your memory.

Summary: Start the guessing process as soon as you decide that you can't answer the question based on your knowledge.

How to Narrow Down the Choices

The next chapter in this book (**Test-Taking Strategies**) includes a wide range of strategies for how to approach questions and how to look for answer choices to eliminate. You will definitely want to read those carefully, practice them, and figure out which ones work best for you. Here though, we're going to address a mindset rather than a particular strategy.

Your odds of guessing an answer correctly depend on how many options you are choosing from.

Number of options left	5	4	3	2	1
Odds of guessing correctly	20%	25%	33%	50%	100%

You can see from this chart just how valuable it is to be able to eliminate incorrect answers and make an educated guess, but there are two things that many test takers do that cause them to miss out on the benefits of guessing:

- Accidentally eliminating the correct answer
- Selecting an answer based on an impression

We'll look at the first one here, and the second one in the next section.

To avoid accidentally eliminating the correct answer, we recommend a thought exercise called **the $5 challenge**. In this challenge, you only eliminate an answer choice from contention if you are willing to bet $5 on it being wrong. Why $5? Five dollars is a small but not insignificant amount of money. It's an amount you could afford to lose but wouldn't want to throw away. And while losing $5 once might not hurt too much, doing it twenty times will set you back $100. In the same way, each small decision you make—eliminating a choice here, guessing on a question there—won't by itself impact your score very much, but when you put them all together, they can make a big difference. By holding each answer choice elimination decision to a higher standard, you can reduce the risk of accidentally eliminating the correct answer.

The $5 challenge can also be applied in a positive sense: If you are willing to bet $5 that an answer choice *is* correct, go ahead and mark it as correct.

Summary: Only eliminate an answer choice if you are willing to bet $5 that it is wrong.

Which Answer to Choose

You're taking the test. You've run into a hard question and decided you'll have to guess. You've eliminated all the answer choices you're willing to bet $5 on. Now you have to pick an answer. Why do we even need to talk about this? Why can't you just pick whichever one you feel like when the time comes?

The answer to these questions is that if you don't come into the test with a plan, you'll rely on your impression to select an answer choice, and if you do that, you risk falling into a trap. The test writers know that everyone who takes their test will be guessing on some of the questions, so they intentionally write wrong answer choices to seem plausible. You still have to pick an answer though, and if the wrong answer choices are designed to look right, how can you ever be sure that you're not falling for their trap? The best solution we've found to this dilemma is to take the decision out of your hands entirely. Here is the process we recommend:

Once you've eliminated any choices that you are confident (willing to bet $5) are wrong, select the first remaining choice as your answer.

Whether you choose to select the first remaining choice, the second, or the last, the important thing is that you use some preselected standard. Using this approach guarantees that you will not be enticed into selecting an answer choice that looks right, because you are not basing your decision on how the answer choices look.

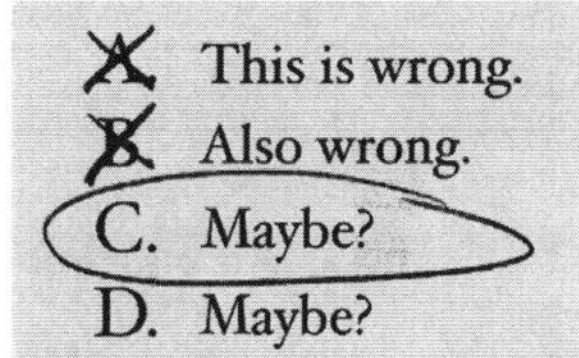

This is not meant to make you question your knowledge. Instead, it is to help you recognize the difference between your knowledge and your impressions. There's a huge difference between thinking an answer is right because of what you know, and thinking an answer is right because it looks or sounds like it should be right.

Summary: To ensure that your selection is appropriately random, make a predetermined selection from among all answer choices you have not eliminated.

Test-Taking Strategies

This section contains a list of test-taking strategies that you may find helpful as you work through the test. By taking what you know and applying logical thought, you can maximize your chances of answering any question correctly!

It is very important to realize that every question is different and every person is different: no single strategy will work on every question, and no single strategy will work for every person. That's why we've included all of them here, so you can try them out and determine which ones work best for different types of questions and which ones work best for you.

Question Strategies

☑ Read Carefully

Read the question and the answer choices carefully. Don't miss the question because you misread the terms. You have plenty of time to read each question thoroughly and make sure you understand what is being asked. Yet a happy medium must be attained, so don't waste too much time. You must read carefully and efficiently.

☑ Contextual Clues

Look for contextual clues. If the question includes a word you are not familiar with, look at the immediate context for some indication of what the word might mean. Contextual clues can often give you all the information you need to decipher the meaning of an unfamiliar word. Even if you can't determine the meaning, you may be able to narrow down the possibilities enough to make a solid guess at the answer to the question.

☑ Prefixes

If you're having trouble with a word in the question or answer choices, try dissecting it. Take advantage of every clue that the word might include. Prefixes can be a huge help. Usually, they allow you to determine a basic meaning. *Pre-* means before, *post-* means after, *pro-* is positive, *de-* is negative. From prefixes, you can get an idea of the general meaning of the word and try to put it into context.

☑ Hedge Words

Watch out for critical hedge words, such as *likely*, *may*, *can*, *sometimes*, *often*, *almost*, *mostly*, *usually*, *generally*, *rarely*, and *sometimes*. Question writers insert these hedge phrases to cover every possibility. Often an answer choice will be wrong simply because it leaves no room for exception. Be on guard for answer choices that have definitive words such as *exactly* and *always*.

☑ Switchback Words

Stay alert for *switchbacks*. These are the words and phrases frequently used to alert you to shifts in thought. The most common switchback words are *but*, *although*, and *however*. Others include *nevertheless*, *on the other hand*, *even though*, *while*, *in spite of*, *despite*, and *regardless of*. Switchback words are important to catch because they can change the direction of the question or an answer choice.

✓ Face Value

When in doubt, use common sense. Accept the situation in the problem at face value. Don't read too much into it. These problems will not require you to make wild assumptions. If you have to go beyond creativity and warp time or space in order to have an answer choice fit the question, then you should move on and consider the other answer choices. These are normal problems rooted in reality. The applicable relationship or explanation may not be readily apparent, but it is there for you to figure out. Use your common sense to interpret anything that isn't clear.

Answer Choice Strategies

✓ Answer Selection

The most thorough way to pick an answer choice is to identify and eliminate wrong answers until only one is left, then confirm it is the correct answer. Sometimes an answer choice may immediately seem right, but be careful. The test writers will usually put more than one reasonable answer choice on each question, so take a second to read all of them and make sure that the other choices are not equally obvious. As long as you have time left, it is better to read every answer choice than to pick the first one that looks right without checking the others.

✓ Answer Choice Families

An answer choice family consists of two (in rare cases, three) answer choices that are very similar in construction and cannot all be true at the same time. If you see two answer choices that are direct opposites or parallels, one of them is usually the correct answer. For instance, if one answer choice says that quantity x increases and another either says that quantity x decreases (opposite) or says that quantity y increases (parallel), then those answer choices would fall into the same family. An answer choice that doesn't match the construction of the answer choice family is more likely to be incorrect. Most questions will not have answer choice families, but when they do appear, you should be prepared to recognize them.

✓ Eliminate Answers

Eliminate answer choices as soon as you realize they are wrong, but make sure you consider all possibilities. If you are eliminating answer choices and realize that the last one you are left with is also wrong, don't panic. Start over and consider each choice again. There may be something you missed the first time that you will realize on the second pass.

✓ Avoid Fact Traps

Don't be distracted by an answer choice that is factually true but doesn't answer the question. You are looking for the choice that answers the question. Stay focused on what the question is asking for so you don't accidentally pick an answer that is true but incorrect. Always go back to the question and make sure the answer choice you've selected actually answers the question and is not merely a true statement.

✓ Extreme Statements

In general, you should avoid answers that put forth extreme actions as standard practice or proclaim controversial ideas as established fact. An answer choice that states the "process should be used in certain situations, if..." is much more likely to be correct than one that states the "process should be discontinued completely." The first is a calm rational statement and doesn't even make a definitive, uncompromising stance, using a hedge word *if* to provide wiggle room, whereas the second choice is far more extreme.

⊘ Benchmark

As you read through the answer choices and you come across one that seems to answer the question well, mentally select that answer choice. This is not your final answer, but it's the one that will help you evaluate the other answer choices. The one that you selected is your benchmark or standard for judging each of the other answer choices. Every other answer choice must be compared to your benchmark. That choice is correct until proven otherwise by another answer choice beating it. If you find a better answer, then that one becomes your new benchmark. Once you've decided that no other choice answers the question as well as your benchmark, you have your final answer.

⊘ Predict the Answer

Before you even start looking at the answer choices, it is often best to try to predict the answer. When you come up with the answer on your own, it is easier to avoid distractions and traps because you will know exactly what to look for. The right answer choice is unlikely to be word-for-word what you came up with, but it should be a close match. Even if you are confident that you have the right answer, you should still take the time to read each option before moving on.

General Strategies

⊘ Tough Questions

If you are stumped on a problem or it appears too hard or too difficult, don't waste time. Move on! Remember though, if you can quickly check for obviously incorrect answer choices, your chances of guessing correctly are greatly improved. Before you completely give up, at least try to knock out a couple of possible answers. Eliminate what you can and then guess at the remaining answer choices before moving on.

⊘ Check Your Work

Since you will probably not know every term listed and the answer to every question, it is important that you get credit for the ones that you do know. Don't miss any questions through careless mistakes. If at all possible, try to take a second to look back over your answer selection and make sure you've selected the correct answer choice and haven't made a costly careless mistake (such as marking an answer choice that you didn't mean to mark). This quick double check should more than pay for itself in caught mistakes for the time it costs.

⊘ Pace Yourself

It's easy to be overwhelmed when you're looking at a page full of questions; your mind is confused and full of random thoughts, and the clock is ticking down faster than you would like. Calm down and maintain the pace that you have set for yourself. Especially as you get down to the last few minutes of the test, don't let the small numbers on the clock make you panic. As long as you are on track by monitoring your pace, you are guaranteed to have time for each question.

⊘ Don't Rush

It is very easy to make errors when you are in a hurry. Maintaining a fast pace in answering questions is pointless if it makes you miss questions that you would have gotten right otherwise. Test writers like to include distracting information and wrong answers that seem right. Taking a little extra time to avoid careless mistakes can make all the difference in your test score. Find a pace that allows you to be confident in the answers that you select.

⊘ Keep Moving

Panicking will not help you pass the test, so do your best to stay calm and keep moving. Taking deep breaths and going through the answer elimination steps you practiced can help to break through a stress barrier and keep your pace.

Final Notes

The combination of a solid foundation of content knowledge and the confidence that comes from practicing your plan for applying that knowledge is the key to maximizing your performance on test day. As your foundation of content knowledge is built up and strengthened, you'll find that the strategies included in this chapter become more and more effective in helping you quickly sift through the distractions and traps of the test to isolate the correct answer.

Now that you're preparing to move forward into the test content chapters of this book, be sure to keep your goal in mind. As you read, think about how you will be able to apply this information on the test. If you've already seen sample questions for the test and you have an idea of the question format and style, try to come up with questions of your own that you can answer based on what you're reading. This will give you valuable practice applying your knowledge in the same ways you can expect to on test day.

Good luck and good studying!

Economic Factors and Business Information

Basic Economic Concepts

Business Cycle

Business cycle refers to the various stages of growth and retraction in an economy. The four stages are as follows: In **contraction**, growth in the economy has begun to slow, and decline sets in. In a **trough**, the decline has ended. The economy is at the bottom of its cycle and will go no lower. Recessions are often seen during the troughs of economic times. In **expansion**, growth is again happening in the economy, and businesses are investing. This stage does not see a stop in growth. The **peak** stage is the very top of the business cycle. Growth has been the norm for so long that many investors overlook plain economic indicators and continue investing at or past the peak to their detriment.

Monetary Policy and Fiscal Policy

Monetary policy is the means by which the monetary authority (central bank, currency board, etc.) regulate the money supply. This affects not only the growth and size of the supply but also in turn the interest rates. Monetary policy in the United States is set by the Federal Reserve Board (FRB). The FRB's policies are primarily executed by affecting short-term interest rates.

The term **fiscal policy** refers to the government's ability to tax its constituency and spend that revenue to affect the economy. In this way, the government is able to affect, if not change, the various stages of the business cycle. Fiscal policy in the United States is determined by lawmakers or Congress.

The key difference between monetary policy and fiscal policy are the organizations regulating each. Monetary policy in the United States is set and enacted by the **Federal Reserve Bank**. Fiscal policy is legislated through **Congress**. Each new piece of fiscal policy must be voted on and passed in Congress. Monetary policy need not be ratified.

Strong Dollar

A **strong dollar** is a dollar (or unit of currency) that can be exchanged for greater amounts of foreign currency than its present value. When a specific country's currency is stronger than other countries' currencies with whom the country transacts business, **imports** tend to be available more cheaply because the country with the stronger currency can exchange it for more of the foreign currency. **Exports** suffer because the country with the weaker currency tends to buy its goods domestically as it does not lose value in currency conversion at home. A strong dollar is not necessarily good for an economy as it tends to slow growth by hindering sales of exports.

Weak Dollar

A **weak dollar** is a dollar (or unit of currency) that can only be exchanged for smaller amounts of foreign currency than its present value. When a specific country's currency is weaker than other countries' currencies with whom the country transacts business, its exports tend to sell more frequently. This is due to the fact that the countries with stronger currencies effectively buy the exports at a discount, given that their currencies are worth more than the selling country. The country with the weaker currency imports less due to the imports requiring more of the weaker currency; thus, the imports sell at a premium. A weak dollar is not necessarily bad for an economy as it tends to stimulate growth by raising demand for exports due to their low cost.

Effect of Global Exchange Rates on Investment Returns

The strength or weakness of the **domestic currency** affects one's investment portfolio, even a portfolio purely comprised of domestic investments. If a given business sells exported goods priced in USD to foreign countries, then a stronger dollar will relatively lower demand for that business's exports. The same is true in reverse for a weaker dollar, which could comparatively increase demand for that business's goods in foreign countries. Besides this, the effect of **exchange rates** for investments held in foreign currencies is more direct, as an increase in the strength of a foreign currency relative to the domestic currency will directly cause that investment's value to increase. This increase or decrease in investment returns due to currency strength can counteract or accelerate the gain or loss of an investment that is more intermingled with the global economy.

Sovereign Debt

Sovereign debt is debt issued by a sovereign government (i.e., not a mere municipality or local government) to foreign issuers, or what might be called **external sovereign debt**. Sovereign debt is characterized by being unsecured, for creditors cannot claim government assets in the event of default. The value of any given sovereign debt depends rather heavily on that nation's particular political and economic milieu, with less stable nations therefore requiring higher interest rates to persuade foreign creditors to invest in them. This can lead to crises, for unlike government debt to domestic creditors, sovereign debtors lack control over the currency in which their debt is denominated, which otherwise allows governments to resolve domestic debt issues.

Inflation and the Relationship of Inflation to GDP

Inflation is the chronologically regular, systematic increase in the money supply or in general price levels. **Gross domestic product (GDP)** consists of the collective total production of a given economy. If the GDP is declining, or even keeping an even pace, the economy is not growing, and companies are not able to expand their profits or benefit investors. Too much growth in GDP, however, is also not good for the economy. Inflation tends to keep pace with GDP. If GDP is racing skyward and inflation paces it, investors' funds are losing purchasing power because of the increase in general price levels.

Deflation is the inverse of inflation. It is a general decline in the price of goods and services usually observed during a period of decline in money supply and credit across the economy. When there is deflation, the purchasing power of currency is increasing. To put it another way, during deflation prices are falling so the same amount of money buys more.

Interest Rates and Yield Curves

Bond values have an inverse relationship to the **yield** the bond pays. In a **rising interest rate** environment, new bonds produce higher yields for the same outlay of principal to the investor. This decreases the demand for existing bonds, and the value falls accordingly. Conversely, in a **falling interest rate** environment, investors are willing to pay more to receive the higher yields produced by existing bonds. Because yield is a function of the amount invested and the coupon received, the **yield curve** also moves with interest rates. Short-term bond values tend not to move as dramatically as long-term bond values due to the fact that they can be redeemed at par value much more quickly and reinvested in higher-yielding securities if interest rates rise. This also results in a lower coupon (less yield) as the interest rate expense is much lower than with long-term bonds. Long-term values (and thus their respective yields), however, tend to be more volatile as they are inflexible due to their longer durations. This volatility results in higher yields being paid. This results in a **normal yield curve**, having an upward sloping shape, with lower yields corresponding to short-term bonds and higher yields corresponding to long-term bonds.

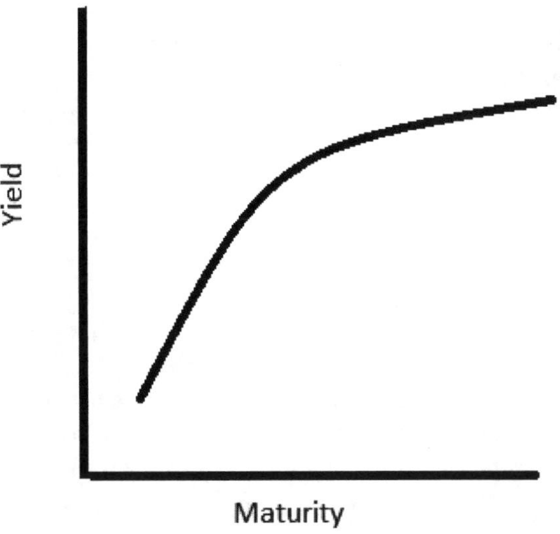

Economic Indicator

Economic indicators are (usually) large-scale economic data used to construe current economic conditions and forecast potential economic conditions. Economic indicators may be taken from multiple sources, but there are generally accepted indicators that provide the most value to investors and economists.

The five most commonly used and generally accepted as the most useful indicators include the following:

1. **GDP**, or gross domestic product, a measure of a nation's total output
2. **Employment indicators**, such as the national unemployment rate
3. **Trade deficit**, or conditions such that a nation's imports exceed its exports
4. **Balance of payments**, or records of dealings between a given country and all other countries with whom it has done business over a particular period of time
5. **CPI**, or consumer price index, a measure of inflation

Financial Reporting

Financial Statements

Financial statements are transcribed reports of a company's financial status. Investors use financial statements to make informed decisions about investing in those companies. There are three main parts to a financial statement. They are the income statement, the balance sheet, and the statement of cash flows.

1. The **income statement**, or profit and loss statement, reports income received during a specified time period versus expenses accounted to that income. It helps the investor determine whether or not the company turned a profit over a period of time.

2. The **balance sheet** is a summated report of a company's assets, liabilities, and owners' equity (or shareholders' equity). It can be summarized with the following equation: assets = liabilities + owners' equity. From this information, an investor should be able to ascertain a clear picture regarding the company's assets, how much (if any) money is owed, and the amount invested by owners or shareholders at a given point in time.
3. The **statement of cash flows** is the financial statement that records the income and outlay of a company's cash. It helps the investor determine if the company has enough cash to meet its regular expenses and acquire new assets. They also help determine whether or not a company is generating cash.

SEC Filings

A company that is publicly traded and listed on any major exchange must be registered with the Securities Exchange Commission and provide regular statements of that company's condition, or financial statements to the SEC. These are known as **SEC filings**. SEC filings provide uniformity (or a certain degree thereof) to multiple companies that make it easier for the investor to understand than the more complex and company-specific statements that a firm may use for its internal accounting and decision making. Securities Exchange Commission filings are also governed by the SEC, which provides extra incentive for the company to report accurate figures to prevent a loss of trading privileges or civil penalties and fines.

Annual Report

An **annual report** is intended to comprehensively summarize a company's activities for investors (and others) over the past year. (**Interim reports** are reports issued more frequently.) Annual reports include financial statements (such as income statements, balance sheets, and statements of cash flows), notes to the financial statements, accounting policies, statements and reports from management, directors, chairmen, and/or auditors, material risk disclosures, and other information.

Auditor Disclosures

Audits ensure that some representation made by a company to a third party or to the public are true and reliable. Audits frequently involve ensuring that the financial statements of a publicly-traded company are reliable for the public to depend on them in making investment decisions, in particular their conformity with GAAP. When auditors investigate the truth and reliability of financial statements, they will **disclose** an opinion on them. The best opinion to be offered is an unqualified (or unmodified) opinion, where the auditor states that in his professional judgment without qualification (or modification), the financial statements represent reality and conform to GAAP. There can also be qualified (or modified) opinions, where the auditor provides a significant but relatively minor qualification to the financial statements' accuracy or reliability, or an adverse opinion, where he discloses a more material error in the financial statements.

Depending on the purposes for which financial statements are utilized, some financial statements—as well as other financial representations which are not broad enough to count as whole financial statements—will be **unaudited**, or perhaps audited only in a less intensive manner (e.g., where the auditor tests for numerical accuracy but not conformity to GAAP).

Different Bases of Financial Accounting

Financial accounting can broadly be distinguished into two forms, cash-basis accounting and accrual-basis accounting. **Cash-basis accounting** is quite commonsense, as it reports events and transactions only when cash is actually disbursed or received by an entity. This stands opposed to **accrual-basis accounting**, where events and transactions are reported only when revenues are earned and expenses incurred. For instance, accrual-basis accounting would record a sale when the customer pledges to pay for a good, while cash-basis accounting would record it only when the customer actually pays. There can also be other bases of accounting, where certain events or transactions are subject to cash-basis rules and others to accrual-basis rules.

Analytical Methods

Time Value of Money Concept

The **time value of money concept** is the assumption that money held today is worth more than money received tomorrow. There are several reasons why this is a valid assumption. The rate of inflation makes future dollars worth less due to the loss in purchasing power. Similarly, money invested tomorrow instead of today also suffers from the loss of potential returns given up. There are several formulas to figure the time value of money dependent upon the type of calculation an investor desires. The time value of money concept is a very important tool as it helps investors decide whether or not an investment is worth undertaking.

IRR

The **internal rate of return (IRR)** is the rate of expected growth. To find IRR, the investor sets the time value of money equation equal to zero. Generally, a higher IRR indicates a higher probability of positive returns. This helps the investor take full advantage of the time value of their money by avoiding underperforming investments. Many companies use IRR to determine whether or not a project is worth undertaking. They will compare the IRR to general rates of return in the financial markets. If none of their proposed projects offer a higher IRR than the rates offered in the market, they have the option of investing the capital in the markets that would have been invested in the project.

NPV

Net present value (NPV) calculations show the value of a dollar today compared to the value of the same dollar in the future, accounting for inflation and returns (subtracting inflation from returns). If the NPV is negative, the investment being analyzed in not worth being pursued. NPV is calculated as a function of the time value of money by applying a discount rate to expected future values within the time value of money equation. This helps the investor understand if the investment is worth the opportunity cost of not purchasing another investment.

Descriptive Statistics

Descriptive statistics are a set of calculated numbers that are used to generalize a set of data. In relation to the securities industry, descriptive statistics tend to measure risk, reward (returns), and the ranges pertaining thereto. These measurements are useful to investors, allowing them to determine if a security matches their risk tolerance and return needs. The most useful descriptive statistics pertaining to the securities industries are the measures of *central tendency* (mean, median, and mode), *range*, *standard deviation*, and *beta* (and its derivatives).

Review Video: Standard Deviation
Visit mometrix.com/academy and enter code: 419469

Measures of Central Tendency

The measures of central tendency are as follows:

1. **Mean** is the average return of all securities in a given portfolio. Mean is very useful as a metric of portfolio analysis in that it provides the investor a look at how the combined portfolio has performed. While the return of one security is useful in determining its validity in a portfolio, it is not useful in gauging the general performance of the entire portfolio and its relative cohesiveness.
2. **Median** is the number representing the return that falls directly in the middle of all other returns of securities in the portfolio. It provides another view of empirical data to be considered with the other measures of central tendency. The median metric also helps the investor understand the impact of an outlier return and act accordingly.
3. **Mode** is the most recurrent return in a portfolio. This measure of central tendency assists the investor in finding trends, positive or negative, and dealing with them appropriately.

Range

Range is the difference in the highest return of the portfolio and the lowest return of the portfolio. It covers all numbers in between. This look at a portfolio's performance allows the investor or adviser to statistically evaluate the range of the included securities. If there is a **large range**, there may or may not be a problem with the portfolio that needs to be addressed, depending on the investors' time horizon and risk appetite. A large range may also be a sign of negative correlation in the portfolio, whereas a smaller range tends to indicate positive correlation. Both of the scenarios can be problematic or show that an investor's strategy is working, again dependent upon time horizon and risk appetite.

Standard Deviation

Standard deviation measures the distance each of the returns in the portfolio falls from the mean. The further spread the data is, the higher the measure of standard deviation. A higher standard deviation then indicates a high degree of volatility and thus risk. It is a very useful metric in determining the suitability of an investment for a client, risk averse or otherwise. Standard deviation may also apply to an individual security by measuring its historical mean performance against the historical returns making up the mean. In this case, too, a higher standard deviation represents a higher amount of volatility and risk.

Beta

Beta is a measure of volatility used to judge the risk of a given security or portfolio. A higher beta indicates a riskier portfolio or security. Beta is a metric showing a security's or portfolio's correlation to market movement. A beta measurement of 1 indicates a 1-for-1 performance tracked against the security's or portfolio's benchmark. A 50 percent decrease in the value of the benchmark of a portfolio or security would also result in a 50 percent decrease in the value of that portfolio or security. Beta measuring 0.50 in the same scenario would result in only a 25 percent decrease in value. Beta's measurement works the same for measurements less than or greater than 1. A measurement above 1 indicates higher volatility and larger value swings. A measurement below 1 indicates lower volatility and lesser value swings.

Alpha

Where Beta is a measure of volatility, **Alpha** is a measure of performance. Alpha is frequently referred to as the abnormal rate of return or excess return, and indicates when an investment has beaten the market over a designated period of time. The return generated by an investment relative to its benchmark is the investment's alpha, which can be positive or negative and is the result of an active investing strategy.

Financial Ratios

Financial ratios are a comparison of two specific numbers taken from financial statements. They provide the investor with quick information to help make an informed decision, but the information they provide is very broad and not entirely precise. While there are many types of financial ratios, the most useful and commonly used are the following:

1. The **debt-to-equity ratio** is a measurement of a company's liabilities (debt) compared to owners' or shareholders' equity. These numbers are located on the balance sheet. The debt-to-equity ratio can be solved using the following equation: debt-to-equity ratio = total liabilities/(owners' or shareholders' equity)
2. The **current ratio**, or liquidity ratio, gives the investor a snapshot of the company's current condition by comparing current assets to current liabilities. This helps determine if the company is capable of meeting short-term obligations (debt and accounts payable) with short-term assets (cash, inventory, and accounts receivable). The equation for the current ratio is current ratio = current assets/current liabilities.

The **quick ratio** helps investors determine short-term liquidity by comparing current assets less inventory to current liabilities. This ratio tends to give a truer picture of the company's condition than the current ratio because it excludes inventory from the equation. Some companies struggle to move inventory, and this can prove problematic when figuring liquidity with the current ratio. The quick ratio is figured as follows: quick ratio = (current assets – inventories)/current liabilities.

Valuation Ratios

Valuation ratios help investors analyze a company's performance in various areas by providing a snapshot glimpse of related data compared to each other. While one valuation ratio is helpful, by itself, it does not provide a clear enough picture to warrant purchasing a security.

1. The **price-to-earnings, or P/E, ratio** helps the investor compare a security's market value (price per share) to the company's earnings per share. It is calculated as market value per share/earnings per share. A higher P/E may indicate that investors predict larger earnings in the future than a company with a lower P/E.
2. The **price-to-book ratio** helps investors compare a company's market value (price per share) to its book value, or a company's value based on its assets versus liabilities listed on the balance sheet. This ratio is a conservative look at the value of the company versus how much the investor is paying per share. It is calculated as price per share/shareholders' equity per share.

Types of Risk

Systematic Risk

Systematic, or **un-diversifiable, risk** is intrinsic to the whole market or market subdivision and may not be negated through diversification. It is also called market risk as it is risk that any investor in the market takes on. Examples of systematic risk range from wars to volatile interest rates.

1. **Market risk** describes the chance that an investor may suffer losses because of dynamics that affect the general performance of the market. An example might be a terrorist attack that results in overall market decline.

2. **Interest rate risk** describes the possibility that an investment may lose value due to changes in the overall interest rates. A large increase in interest rates can adversely affect bond portfolios.
3. **Inflation risk** describes the risk that an investor's investments' return will not keep pace with inflation and that he will ultimately lose purchasing power because of it.

Unsystematic Risk

Unsystematic risk can be defined as specific risk, in that it is specific to certain factors of the investment, such as the industry. A shipping concern off the coast of Somalia may experience piracy as an unsystematic risk. Unsystematic risk may be described as diversifiable risk as it may be overcome through the diversification of a portfolio.

1. **Business risk** describes the risk that a business will have worse-than-expected profits or that it will record a loss instead of a profit.
2. **Regulatory risk** describes the risk that the regulatory environment will negatively impact an industry. Stricter gun control laws are an example of regulatory risk to the firearms industry.
3. **Political risk** differs from regulatory risk in that it describes the risk that ensues from political upheaval or instability and unrest in a country. An example of this is an oil company being nationalized after a political revolution.
4. **Liquidity risk** is the risk that an investor will not be able to liquidate or receive cash for the investment in a timely manner.

Opportunity Cost

Opportunity cost is the potential benefits ceded from one opportunity in order to pursue another opportunity. While this may seem ambiguous, investors may think of it in concrete terms. To investors, opportunity cost may be the return given up on other investments when they choose a specific investment. If their chosen investment returns less than another investment, then they suffered a **measurable opportunity cost** measured by the differences in the returns. If, however, the investment purchased has greater returns, the opportunity cost is **negative** and not real.

Opportunity cost is unavoidable because, to purchase an investment, an investor must forgo the potential benefit of any other investment that he or she may have purchased with that particular amount of capital.

Capital Structure and Order of Liquidation Priority

Capital structure is the term given to the method by which a company finances its operations. It is some combination of long and short-term debt and preferred and common stock issued. Capital structure is often referred to in conjunction with the debt-to-equity ratio. Capital structure differs vastly from company to company. Companies that are highly **leveraged**, that is, most of their capital comes from borrowing funds through bonds and notes, are considered much riskier than companies that raise most of their capital through equity issuance and sales. This results in an expectation of higher return on investment to compensate for the greater risk taken.

In the unfortunate event of bankruptcy and liquidation of the firm's assets, after the general creditors have been repaid, the order of **liquidation**, or the order in which the security holders are reimbursed, is as follows:

1. secured debtors (secured bonds)
2. unsecured debtors (unsecured bonds)

3. preferred stockholders
4. common stockholders

Economic Factors and Business Information Chapter Quiz

1. An investor should go to defensive stocks at what point of the business cycle?

a. The Expansion phase
b. The Peak phase
c. The Contraction phase
d. The Trough phase

2. Monetary policy tools, used by the Federal Reserve, primarily are:

a. The reserve requirement
b. Open Market operations
c. The discount rate
d. All of the above

3. Which is a primary risk to an investor's "purchasing power"?

a. Low interest rates
b. Equity volatility
c. Inflation
d. Deflation

4. In an environment of steadily rising interest rates, the average investor looking to preserve capital should avoid which of the following investments?

a. Real estate investment trusts
b. Long term bonds
c. Short term bonds
d. Large cap stocks

5. In a situation where short-term interest rates are higher than longer term interest rates, which of the following is true?

a. The yield curve is inverted and is an indicator of positive economic growth
b. The yield curve is normal and is an indicator of positive economic growth
c. The yield curve is inverted and is an indicator of negative economic growth
d. The yield curve is normal and is an indicator of negative economic growth

6. On an income statement, all of the following would be factored into the gross margin except which of the following?

a. Operating expenses
b. Cost of goods sold
c. Sales revenue
d. Packaging

7. On a balance sheet, assets are generally one of three types. Which of the following is not a type of asset found on a balance sheet?

a. Current assets
b. Fixed assets
c. Saleable assets
d. Intangible assets

8. Calculating the Net Present Value (NPV) is useful in which of the following situations?

a. Comparing a bond investment to a stock investment
b. Deciding whether a business investment is a good use of cash
c. Deciding which of two mutual funds is a better investment
d. Comparing an investment in a preferred stock to a common stock

9. Which of the following mutual funds would you most like to invest in?

a. The one with the highest standard deviation
b. The one with the highest Sharpe ratio
c. The one with the highest Sortino ratio
d. The one with the highest positive Alpha

10. Emerging markets equity investors generally don't have to worry about which of the following risks?

a. Reinvestment risk
b. Political risk
c. Currency risk
d. Opportunity cost

Economic Factors and Business Information Chapter Quiz Answers

1. B: The peak phase is where cyclical stocks are popular and richly valued. At that time defensive stocks are cheaper and should hold their value better through the contraction phase.

2. D: All of the above. All of these, and more, are the tools the Fed uses to "tighten" or "loosen" money in its attempts to reduce unemployment and fight inflation.

3. C: Inflation. Over time, inflationary forces cause prices to increase, thereby causing the value of what a "dollar" will buy to decrease. For example, movie theater tickets have risen consistently over time so that the same movie experience can now cost 3x what it did twenty years ago.

4. B: Long term bonds are the most vulnerable to rising interest rates. REITs and stocks fare the best in a rising rate environment and the shorter duration of short-term bonds get hurt much less than long term bonds.

5. C: The situation of short-term rates being higher than longer term rates is not normal, and is therefore inverted. This is often a predictor of negative economic growth and is viewed by some as a recession indicator.

6. A: Operating expenses are not considered in calculating gross margin, but are factored into the operating margin.

7. C: Saleable assets would be included in inventory which is a current asset.

8. B: NPV is relevant when calculating future cash flows and whether the cost of current investment will be returned in future increased cash flows or not.

9. D: A fund that consistently has positive Alpha is a winner. Usually this is best when risk is taken into account. You can get a higher overall return by taking more risk, but there may be no Alpha at all and that really hurts in a down market.

10. A: Typically, EM equities are invested in simply for capital appreciation, not income. Income investors tend to prefer much less volatility than is normal in emerging markets.

Investment Vehicle Characteristics

Types and Characteristics of Cash & Cash Equivalents

Insured Deposits

Insured deposits are those deposits that are held as cash in a bank or credit union that are insured against loss by another company. For banks, that insuring company is the **Federal Deposit Insurance Corporation**, or the FDIC. The insurance of deposits held at credit unions are insured by the independent federal government agency the National Credit Union Administration, or the NCUA. Insured deposits are cash deposits that may or may not receive interest payments. The interest rates received are usually very low and not comparable to market returns but are generally considered very safe due to the insurance thereon and inability to lose value due to market fluctuations. Given the cash nature of insured deposits, they are liquid deposits. The most illiquid of the deposits are certificates of deposit as early withdrawal will usually result in a forfeiture of some amount of the interest earned. The two types of insured deposit accounts are **demand deposit accounts** and **certificates of deposit**.

Demand Deposits

Demand deposit accounts are most closely associated with checking and savings accounts. The name **demand deposit** refers to the liquidity of the instrument. The deposit may be "demanded" at any time without advanced notice from the depositor. While an investor may receive a small amount of interest on a deposit in a demand deposit account, it is not suitable for any long period as the rate of interest paid usually does not exceed inflation, thereby losing purchasing power in the long run. They are useful, however, due to their totally liquid nature. A retiree may find them very useful in the event that he or she needs quick access to funds for a major life event, given the fact that their time horizon is much smaller than a person in the workforce saving for retirement, thus preventing much loss of purchasing power due to inflation.

Certificate of Deposit

Certificates of deposit (CDs) take the form of savings certificates promising the holder of the CD a specific rate of interest. These savings certificates are cash deposits and therefore liquid and insured by the Federal Deposit Insurance Corporation. If a certificate is redeemed before the maturity date, however, there is usually some forfeiture of interest earned. CDs are characterized by maturity dates and a fixed rate of interest. They are issued in any denomination, but there is usually a minimum deposit stated at the bank's discretion. They are useful to investors who are risk averse but seek some return in the form of interest payments. The interest received on CDs is typically low and tied to prime and in some cases do not keep pace with inflation. They tend to be ideal investments for retirees who are seeking a safe place to invest their funds without the need for much return.

Money Market Instruments

Money market instruments belong to the fixed income sector of the market because they are short maturity debts issued by governments, large companies, and financial institutions. Money market instruments differ from bonds in that they are subject to a much shorter duration for the debt, specifically less than a year. Because of their short duration and relative safety, money market instruments are very liquid. These attractive qualities, however, lend to a low rate of return on money market securities. The two most common and most useful types of money market instruments are **commercial paper** and **Treasury bills**, or T-bills.

Commercial Paper

Commercial paper is a money market instrument characterized by a short duration and an unsecured nature. They are loans that large corporations use to finance accounts receivable and inventory. Commercial paper maturities typically go no longer than nine months, with the average maturity being one to two months. Commercial paper is considered a very safe investment due to the fact that a company's financial situation is easy to forecast in such a short time period. Further adding to their safety is that, usually, commercial paper is only issued by corporations of low risk that show strong stability. Investors find these characteristics to be highly attractive, but the high demand and low risk result in a low interest rate paid on funds invested in commercial paper. Typically, commercial paper is issued in denominations of $100,000, which limits investor access. Smaller investors are able to access commercial paper investments by investing in money market funds.

Treasury Bills

Treasury bills, commonly referred to as **T-bills**, are short-term debt issued by the United States government. They are most commonly issued with maturities of one month, three months, and six months. T-bills are issued in denominations of $1,000 dollars. The greatest amount of T-bills purchasable at one time is $5 million. Treasury bills are issued at a discount to par and redeemed at par by the US government. This differs from traditional debt securities in that no interest payments are made on the debt instrument. The effective interest rate earned is calculated using the difference in the price paid at issue and the price at which the Treasury bills are redeemed. Treasury bills are very safe investments and considered liquid. It is for this reason that they are considered **money market securities**. The relative safety (due to being backed by the US government) and liquidity of Treasury bills make them highly desirable and result in low rates of return, as will other money market instruments.

Types of Fixed Income Securities

Treasury Securities

Treasury bills are short-term debt instruments issued by the United States government with a maturity of less than one year. They are issued at a discount to par and fall into the money market instruments category.

Treasury notes are medium-term debt obligations issued by the United States government. Maturity dates range between one and ten years. They are issued at par value with a fixed rate of interest and fall in the fixed income sector of the market. The fixed interest rate is determined through a competitive bidding process. There is high demand for Treasury notes in the secondary market, making them very liquid.

Treasury bonds, or **T-bonds**, bear the longest maturity of any of the Treasury securities. T-bonds are issued at par with fixed interest and maturities of greater than ten years. The fixed interest rate is determined through a competitive bidding process. Treasury bonds are backed by the full faith and credit of the United States government, making them some of the safest bonds available to investors.

FNMA

FNMA stands for **Federal National Mortgage Association** and is often pronounced "Fannie Mae." It is a government-sponsored, publicly traded company whose goal it is to make homeownership possible for lower-income families. The FNMA was founded in 1938 to create a secondary mortgage market. FNMA buys and guarantees mortgages that meet its underwriting criteria, thus creating mortgage-backed securities. These mortgage-backed securities are resold and tradable. There is a large market for FNMA mortgage-backed securities, making them very liquid. Their liquidity and relative safety (being a government-backed company) make them highly desirable to multiple classes of investors.

TIPS

Treasury Inflation Protected Securities, or TIPS, are debt securities that are issued by the United States government. TIPS are inflation protected in that they are indexed to the current consumer price index (CPI) to prevent loss of purchasing power due to inflation. The par value of TIPS increases each time the CPI rises, while the fixed interest remains constant. TIPS are considered very safe investments as they are backed by the United States government. TIPS fall in the fixed income sector of the market and are attractive to those saving for retirement as they protect against the loss of purchasing power of today's dollars.

Government Agency Bonds

Government agency bonds are not the same as US Treasury or municipal bonds, but pertain to agencies of the federal government. (They also can pertain to quasi-governmental agencies, which are privately operated though either being originally part of the federal government or being sponsored by the federal government.) They are not guaranteed in the same way that Treasury securities are.

Actual **federal agencies** authorized to issue debt securities are the Farm Credit Administration and the Government National Mortgage Association (GNMA, or Ginnie Mae). **Quasi-governmental agencies** authorized to issue debt securities are: Federal Home Loan Mortgage Corporation (FHLMC, or Freddie Mac), Federal National Mortgage Association (FNMA, or Fannie Mae), and Student Loan Marketing Association (SLMA, or Sallie Mae). Except for Ginnie Mae, securities offered by these agencies are not backed by the full faith and credit of the US government, so they pay higher interest than Treasury securities, though lower interest than private bonds.

Governmentally and Corporately Backed Bonds

Governmentally backed bonds are bonds that are secured by a specific government's ability to tax its constituency. This usually results in a very safe, highly rated investment. If, however, the government or the region is unstable, there is greater risk of default by the government.

Corporately backed bonds are secured by a company's ability to perform well in its sector of the market and show that it is profitable. This results in safe, highly rated debt instruments for well-established, large companies that have historically shown their ability to be profitable and repay their debts. By the same token, when small, unproven companies issue debt, it is usually considered highly speculative and risky.

ABSs

Asset-backed securities (ABSs) are securities which are backed with some sort of asset as collateral. The collateralized asset may be loans, leases, receivables, royalties, and other things. Asset-backed securities offer an alternative for many investors to corporate bonds.

Bonds

Bonds are debt instruments issued by corporations to raise capital to finance new ventures and current operations within the company. They are issued at par value, typically $1,000 per bond, and have varying terms to maturity. Bonds are typically issued with a fixed rate of interest, or **coupon**. This coupon is paid in full annually to the holder of the bond. Bonds that are not issued with a coupon are usually issued at a discount to par value and then redeemed at par value. Retirees and those investors looking for current income often rely on **coupon bonds** to meet these needs. Highly rated coupon bonds are generally less volatile than stocks and offer annual income. This meets two of the investor's needs, capital preservation and current income. The low volatility of bonds also makes them popular in long-term investment portfolios as a way to hedge against falling stock prices.

Municipal Bonds

There are four main types of municipal bonds, categorized according to the way that the bond repayments can be financed.

General obligation (GO) bonds are the first type. These are issued to pay for improvements that benefit a community, but don't produce income. They are also known as "full faith and credit issues," because they are repaid from tax revenue raised by the issuing government entity.

Revenue bonds are issued by governments to finance projects and facilities that are expected to generate enough revenue to pay bondholders back without resorting to tax money.

Double-barreled bonds are revenue bonds that also have the backing of the taxing authority. They are considered GO bonds, even though they depend primarily on revenue generated from the project for repayment.

Insured municipal bonds are municipal bonds issued with interest and principal payments guaranteed by a commercial insurance company. Muni bonds are typically considered relatively safe investments due to being issued by local governments, but there is always the possibility that an unexpected event could occur that prevent the issuer from making principal and interest payments. Because this insurance feature reduces the perceived risk of the investment, insured municipal bonds usually lower the yield and rate. However, one additional source of potential risk is the company insuring the bonds, as a company experiencing financial difficulties would be considered less likely to fulfill any payment responsibility that may fall upon them than a company in good financial condition.

Additional Risk When Purchasing Foreign Bonds

Investors that purchase bonds in foreign countries take on many additional **risks**. The additional risk accepted varies by country. In a country characterized by stability and wealth, the additional risks are minimal. In these counties, the additional risk is usually found in the form of political, legislative, and cultural risk, with the first two forms also being present in the United States. **Cultural risk** addresses the ways in which a culture different than that of the United States views business, particularly their views on debt instruments. Investors must also navigate the complex **tax codes** of these countries. In developing or unstable countries, investors are presented with the additional risk of **government instability and revolution** and dependent upon the political system, seizure, and nationalization of private industry.

Advantages When Purchasing Foreign Bonds

Investors purchasing **foreign bonds** accept higher risk when doing so than when purchasing domestic bonds. As with any security purchase, accepting higher risk results in being rewarded with greater returns. Foreign bonds, especially those in developing markets, tend to pay **higher rates of interest** than similar bonds purchased in the United States. Investors also benefit from a **tax deduction** calculated based on the amount of foreign tax associated with their investment that they may have paid to the foreign government. Foreign bonds issued in the United States are issued on the domestic market by a foreign company. This gives the investor exposure to foreign markets without exposing them to risk associate with currency exchange as they are typically issued in United States dollars.

Brady Bonds

Brady bonds are bonds issued **developing countries**, usually by the governments of Latin American nations. Brady bonds derive their name from former United States Treasury Secretary Nicholas Brady. Brady was a major advocate for the reformation of emerging market debt issues for investors from the United States. Brady bonds are useful in that Brady bond transaction activity and demand provide a relevant and informed view of investor appetite for securities and debt instruments issued by emerging markets and developing countries. This helps investors with differing investment goals decide whether or not foreign debt is in line with their investing objectives.

Implications Associated with Investing in Foreign Governmental Debt

Investors in the **governmental debt of foreign countries** should be cautious. Foreign countries are often characterized by cultures with which investors from the United States are not familiar. This can result in political and legislative risk to which the investor is unaccustomed. An **unstable foreign government debt** issue offers additional risk. If the government experiences revolution, the new government may refuse to honor the debts of the previous leadership. Also, investors in foreign government debt must deal with a tax code different than the domestic United States tax code. The ideal investor for foreign government debt ranges according to risk appetite and needs. An investor seeking exposure to foreign markets, but who is also risk averse, may purchase foreign sovereign debt from a stable, long-standing government. Investors seeking capital appreciation and high interest payments may target governments in developing markets as the investors are more capable of absorbing loss but want maximum return.

Foreign Corporate Bonds

Investors seeking exposure to foreign debt markets may target **corporate debt** to maximize their return for capital outlay. While this is an effective method to diversify a portfolio, there are also additional risks inherent to investing in the debt issues of foreign corporations. Foreign corporations are subject to different laws than companies participating in domestic debt markets. Also of unique consideration is the sociopolitical environment of the region. Social unrest can quickly derail production in a company and affect its ability to honor its debts. Investors should also be aware that an unstable government in a foreign market can lead to unfavorable outcomes. A previously business-friendly government may be replaced by a government characterized by central planning, leading to private businesses being nationalized and the possibility that their debt will not be honored.

Characteristics and Valuation Factors of Fixed Income Securities

Taxation of Bonds

Bondholders' income normally comes from the periodic interest payments of the bond. However, discounts and premiums make things slightly more complicated. For tax purposes, any discount on a bond has to be **accreted** (increased) on a straight-line basis over the bond's term; the annual accretion amount is then added to the investor's reported income on the bond. The opposite occurs for bonds purchased at a premium. Premiums are **amortized** (decreased), with the annual amortization amount being subtracted from the investor's reported income.

For example, suppose an investor purchased at 95 a 10-year bond with a face value of $1,000 and stated rate of 6%. The discount of $50 would be accreted at a rate of $5 per year, and so the bondholder's reported income for each year would be $65 ($60 interest + $5 accretion).

Bonds that are originally issued at a discount are unsurprisingly called **original issue discounts** (OIDs).

Bond Rating

The three major **bond rating** agencies are Moody's, Standard and Poor's (S&P), and Fitch. Bonds are graded at issue. Occasionally, the major rating agencies will reevaluate their bond grade and the grade they assigned the issuing company to determine if an upgrade or downgrade is warranted. Investors seeking exposure to the fixed income market use these ratings to help determine which bond is appropriate for their investing needs. An investor with the goal of capital preservation will most likely choose a highly rated bond such as the AAA rating issued by S&P. Investors who are seeking higher income and are less concerned with capital preservation may choose a lower-grade bond that is still investment grade. **Investment grade bonds** are bonds that are considered relatively safe investments. Speculators may choose to invest in **high-yield** or **junk bonds** (BB+ and lower as graded by S&P) to receive the high interest payments or in hopes that a bond purchased at a large discount will appreciate.

Discuss some factors that affect a bond's liquidity.

The following affect **bond liquidity**:

- how well-known or widely owned they are
- the bond rating (higher rating → easier trades)
- the quality of the bond issuer
- how mature the bond is
- how high the interest rate is
- whether it is trading at, above, or below par
- whether it has any call features

Callable Bond

A **callable**, or redeemable, bond is one that the issuer can redeem before it reaches maturity. This allows them to pay off the debt early. The issuer of callable bonds might choose to exercise this right if interest rates are falling so they can re-borrow at a more attractive rate. This is done by issuing the new bonds and using the proceeds to pay off the original debt. In exchange for this, callable bonds typically offer more attractive rates to investors than non-callable bonds when issued. The disadvantage to investors is that while they enjoy higher interest at the outset, if the bond is called they face the prospect of trying to replace it in an environment of lower rates, and therefore lower income.

Coupon Bonds

Coupon bonds are debt instruments that are issued at par and pay a fixed rate of interest to the investor. This rate of interest is known as the **coupon**. A bond issued at a time of high interest rates will be very valuable during times of low interest rates, given that the rate is fixed and the coupon paid is based upon that rate, and coupons paid on new bond issues are based upon the lower rate. Retirees and those investors looking for income often rely on coupon bonds to meet these needs. Highly rated coupon bonds are generally less volatile than stocks and offer annual income. This meets two of the investor's needs, capital preservation and current income.

Zero Coupon Bonds

Zero coupon bonds are bonds which sell at a discounted price because they do not pay interest. The bond is sold at less than face value but is repaid at face value when it reaches maturity. Zero coupon bonds generally have long-term maturities ranging from ten to twenty years. Zero coupon bonds have a higher rate of **price fluctuation** on the open market than regular bonds. The advantage of zero coupon bonds is that an investor can pay a small amount of money up front which will grow into a much larger sum over time. This allows the investor to plan for a future goal like retirement or sending a child to college.

Traditional Bonds and Convertible Bonds

Traditional bonds are issued at par value at some fixed rate of interest. The value of the bond may fluctuate during the period between issue and maturity due to changing interest rate environments, but it will be redeemed at par value at the end of the term. **Convertible bonds** are issued at par value at some fixed rate of interest and provide current income to the holder but may be exchanged at some point for stock in the issuing company and not redeemed at par value. This allows the holder to receive current income similarly to traditional bonds but leaves the option open to participate in gains in the company's stock price. Investors "pay" for this attractive option, however, by collecting a lower coupon.

Bond Premium

The term **bond premium** describes the amount over par value an investor is willing to pay for a bond. In a decreasing interest rate environment, bonds that pay a higher coupon than the current rate are in high demand. This increased demand leads investors who are seeking a higher current income to offer a premium price above par value for the bond with the higher coupon rate. This is a contributing factor in the valuation of a bond. If a bond is held to maturity and a premium was paid for that bond, it may only be redeemed for par value and will result in a capital loss. **Capital appreciation** should not be a goal for those who invest in bonds at a premium. The main objective for premium bond buying should be **higher current income**.

Buying and Selling Bonds at a Discount

Buying bonds at a **discount** is the practice of investors paying less than par value for a bond. The reason a bond might be valued at less than par is in rising interest rate environments where bonds paying the old, lower rate of interest are not in demand. Because an investor will not pay par value to receive a lower rate of interest for a similar bond, bond sellers discount the prices of the bonds they hold to make them more attractive to investors. The lower outlay of capital in conjunction with the lower coupon helps investors to receive similar yield to the new bonds with higher rates of interest. This is a contributing factor in the valuation of a bond. **Capital appreciation** at maturity is attainable with these bonds as they will be redeemed at par value and were bought at a discount to par. Some bonds are issued at a discount and do not pay interest payments. The perceived interest earned is realized when the investor holds the bond until maturity and receives the par value. The increase in the value of a bond bought in this method is called **accretion**.

Bond Duration

Bond duration is a product of multiple factors related to bonds and their issues. The factors used to calculate bond duration are the net present value, yield, coupon, final maturity, and call features. Bond duration is measured in years and addresses interest rate risk related to the maturity of the bond. All of the previously stated factors are used in a complex formula to determine the bond duration. Duration gives the investor an idea of the **value** of a bond based on whether interest rates increase or decline. Longer duration periods tend to make the value of the bond **fluctuate** more because of the fluid nature of interest rates. Bond duration can also be a measure of volatility based on interest rate movements and the maturity of the bond.

MATURITY

Maturity terms are the effective length of debt instruments, particularly bonds. When a debt instrument is issued at par value with a fixed interest rate, it is also assigned a **maturity date**. For the length of time until maturity, the issuing entity promises to pay the fixed rate. Bonds may then trade on the secondary market at a discount or premium to par until maturity. At maturity, the issuing entity redeems the bond at par value and is no longer obligated to pay the fixed rate. **Duration** is a function of maturity that uses the bond's maturity as part of the calculation. While duration and maturity are both usually measured in years, a bond's duration may be longer or shorter than its time to maturity based upon the bond's net present value, yield, coupon, maturity, and call features.

TAXATION

Gains from investments on municipal bonds are ordinarily not taxed. **Taxable municipal bonds** can be issued if the purpose of the bond revenue has no clear public benefit, but most municipal bonds are **tax-exempt**.

This means not only that coupon payments are not taxed, but also that gains from original issue discount (OID) bonds are tax-exempt as well. Accretion on the discount of municipal OID bonds is treated as tax-exempt interest income.

Discounts on municipal bonds purchased in the secondary market are not even accreted. These are the only bonds whose discounts are not accreted.

TAX-EQUIVALENT YIELD

The **tax-equivalent yield** is the yield that a taxable bond needs to have before taxes in order to achieve the same return as a nontaxable bond.

Tax-equivalent yield = (desired yield) / (1 – tax rate)

For example, if a nontaxable bond had a yield of 18% and the tax rate were 12%, then any taxable bonds, to be more valuable to the investor, would need to have a yield of 20.45% (18% / 88%).

EXAMPLE 1

An investor with a marginal tax rate of 28% is trying to decide whether to add Bond A or Bond B to his portfolio. If the only factor that he will be considering is yield, which is the better choice?

Bond A: Corporate Bond with an annual coupon rate of 5%

Bond B: Municipal Bond with an annual coupon rate of 4%

Determine the after-tax yield for the municipal bond and then compare to the corporate bond rate.

$$Tax\ Equivalent\ Yield = \frac{Yield\ of\ Muni\ Bond}{(1 - Tax\ Rate)}$$

$$Tax\ Equivalent\ Yield\ for\ Bond\ B = \frac{4\%}{(1 - .28)} = 5.56\%$$

5.56% > 5%, so Bond B has a higher tax-equivalent yield.

Federal, State, and Local Taxation for Municipal Bonds

Investors need not pay any taxes on **interest income** from municipal bonds, although they may have to pay state or local taxes, depending on their laws.

US territories (including American Samoa, Guam, Puerto Rico, and the Virgin Islands) and federal districts (Washington, D.C.) are **triple tax-free** regarding municipal bonds. Bondholders don't have any federal, state, or local taxes to pay on interest.

Most states, but not all, are triple tax-free regarding municipal bonds for investors purchasing bonds issued within their own state.

Despite all these tax exemptions for interest income, capital gains from the sales of bonds is still taxable.

Relationship Between Bond Valuation and Interest Rates

The value of a bond fluctuates in relation to the **yield** it produces. Bond values have an inverse relationship to the yield the bond pays. In a **rising interest rate environment**, new bonds produce higher yields for the same outlay of principal to the investor. This decreases the demand for existing bonds, and the value falls accordingly. Conversely, in a **falling interest rate environment**, investors are willing to pay more to receive the higher yields produced by existing bonds. Long-term bonds are more susceptible to this form of interest rate risk than short-term bonds. Short-term bonds may be redeemed at par value and reinvested in a higher-yielding security within a shorter time frame than long-term bonds. A two-year duration of receiving subpar yields is much more palatable than thirty years of subpar yields.

Example 1

Calculate the modified duration for a bond with the following properties, if interest rates were to increase by 1%.

Macaulay Duration = 5 years
Yield to Maturity = 5%
1 Coupon Payment Per year

The modified duration is 4.76 years.

Example 2

A bond offers a yield to maturity of 3% and makes coupon payments semi-annually. You are told that a 1% increase in interest rates would lead to a modified duration of exactly 8 years. What is the current duration?

The current duration is 8.12 years.

Yield-to-Call

Yield-to-call as related to the bond market is only applicable to callable bonds. **Callable bonds** are those bonds that are issued with a clause stating times and conditions that a bond may be called back from investors, or redeemed early. These bonds are characterized by the additional risks of call risk, or the risk that the bond will be called before maturity, and investment risk, or finding a suitable investment to replace the investment called away. These bonds tend to pay higher fixed rates as they contain more inherent risk and are less attractive to buyers. Low demand for callable bonds results in a lower valuation. Investors seeking high income also tend to value callable bonds lowly because the actual yield of the bond is affected negatively by the call date. This concept embodies yield-to-call.

EXAMPLE

Calculate the yield to call for a callable bond with the following characteristics:

$1,000 par
2% coupon (pays annually)
$800 market price
callable 2 years from now
103% call premium

Where:

P = current price of bond
n = number of periods until call
c = coupon payment
C = call price
r = rate of return (i.e., yield to call)
t = number of periods until call

$$800 = \sum_{t=1}^{2} \frac{20}{(1+r)^t} + \frac{1030}{(1+r)^2}$$

$$800 = \frac{20}{(1+r)^1} + \frac{20}{(1+r)^2} + \frac{1030}{(1+r)^2}$$

$$800(1+r)^2 = 20(1+\text{r}) + 20 + 1030$$

$$800(1+r)^2 = 20\text{r} + 1070$$

$$800(r^2 + 2r + 1) = 20\text{r} + 1070$$

$$800r^2 + 1600r + 800 = 20\text{r} + 1070$$

$$800r^2 + 1580r - 270 = 0$$

$$\text{r} = 15.82\%$$

YIELD-TO-MATURITY

The **yield-to-maturity**, or **YTM**, of a bond is a characteristic that applies to all bonds. YTM is a function of the price an investor paid for a bond (whether at issue, a premium, or discount), the fixed rate of interest paid, and the time left to maturity. A bond purchased at a discount will have a higher YTM than a bond purchased at a premium or at par if the bonds have the same fixed rate of interest and date of maturity. YTM will help an investor to decide if there is more benefit to buying a bond at a large discount with a small coupon versus a bond with a high coupon bond, which will require a large premium to obtain.

EXAMPLE

ABC Medical is a $1,000 par 8% coupon (pays semiannually) bond selling at $950. The bond matures one year from now. Calculate the yield to maturity.

Where:

P = current price of bond
n = number of periods until call
c = coupon payment
F = face value
r = rate of return
t = number of periods until call

$$950 = \sum_{t=1}^{2} \frac{40}{(1+r)^t} + \frac{1000}{(1+r)^2}$$

$$950 = \frac{40}{(1+r)^1} + \frac{40}{(1+r)^2} + \frac{1000}{(1+r)^2}$$

$$950(1+r)^2 = 40(1+\mathrm{r}) + 40 + 1000$$

$$950(1+r)^2 = 40\mathrm{r} + 1080$$

$$950(r^2 + 2r + 1) = 40\mathrm{r} + 1080$$

$$950r^2 + 1900r + 950 = 40\mathrm{r} + 1080$$

$$950r^2 + 1860r - 130 = 0$$

$$\mathrm{r} = 6.76\%$$

The YTM will be 6.76% × 2 = 13.51%, for the semiannual coupon payments make 2r to be the annualized rate of return in this example.

Coupon of a Bond

The **coupon of a bond** is the fixed rate of interest paid to the investor holding the bond. A **high coupon** is very attractive for an investor seeking current income. In low interest rate environments, high coupon bonds command a premium due to the fact that the investor is seeking higher income and cannot find it in the low interest rate environment. It is a classic example of supply and demand. The supply of **low coupon bonds** in low interest rate environments is plentiful because they are being issued regularly. The supply of high coupon bonds in low interest rate environments is scarce because of those investors seeking higher income. The supply-and-demand relationship causes the value of the high coupon bonds to increase. This relationship exhibited between interest rates, or the coupon, and the value of bonds is an inverse relationship; as one increases, the other declines.

Implications of Valuing Convertible Bonds

Convertible bonds differ from conventional bonds in that they may be converted from debt instruments to equity securities by the investor. Convertible bonds are attractive to investors because they provide investments in the more stable bond market while providing the investor with the opportunity to participate in the equity gains of a company should it begin to perform well. While this is an attractive option for the investor, it comes with a price. Because of this advantage, **lower coupons** are offered on convertible bonds. Lower coupons result in lower valuations of the bonds because they don't provide as much current income as may be available in other debt instruments.

Effect of Rating on Valuation

The **risk/reward theory** states that an investment that bears high risk should return high rewards to be worth accepting the risk associated with the investment. While this results in risky bonds commanding high coupon payments, or fixed interest payments, the inherent risk diminishes the attractiveness of the bond to investors looking to bonds for capital preservation. This causes investors with different investing needs to value the bonds differently. While bonds that are rated lowly may be very attractive to a young investor looking to take on risk to help his or her savings grow, they may be eschewed by the retiree seeking to preserve his or her capital.

Credit Spread for Bonds

Credit spread is the difference in value between two bonds with different credit ratings that are otherwise identical, with the comparison often made in comparison to a US Treasury bond, as such a bond is deemed to be maximally secure. Credit spread is measured or stated in terms of **basis points**, each point equal to a hundredth of one percent, and all with reference to the bonds' yield. For example, if a proposed 5-year corporate bond had a yield of 3.89% and the corresponding 5-year US Treasury bond had a yield of 2.36%, then the credit spread for these two bonds would be 389 - 236 = 153 basis points.

Discounted Cash Flow

Discounted cash flow as related to fixed income securities is a function of present value calculations. To calculate the discounted cash flow of a bond, the investor should apply the net present value formula to all expected cash flows from the bond (i.e., fixed interest payments) using the rate of inflation as the discount rate. This effectively provides the investor with a measurement of the **time value of money**. Investors use discounted cash flow in their evaluation of bonds by applying the time value discounts to their overall return on investment in today's dollars. If a bond has a very long maturity, at some point, the fixed interest payments may not be enough to justify today's expenditure of capital. This would devalue the bond and make it less attractive.

Example 1

Calculate the discounted cash flow for a $100,000 future cash flow payable in 10 years using a discount rate of 5%.

Where:

CF= cash flow
r = discount rate
n = number of payments

$$Discounted\ Cash\ Flow = \frac{100{,}000}{(1+.05)^{10}}$$

$Discounted\ Cash\ Flow = \$61{,}391$

EXAMPLE 2

Calculate the discounted cash flow for a $1,000,000 future cash flow payable in 5 years using a discount rate of 7%.

Where:

CF= cash flow
r = discount rate
n = number of payments

$$Discounted\ Cash\ Flow = \frac{1{,}000{,}000}{(1 + .07)^5}$$

$$Discounted\ Cash\ Flow = \$712{,}986$$

Describe the characteristics of equity securities and their role in portfolio allocation.

EQUITY SECURITIES

Equity securities, most commonly referred to as **stocks**, are sold as individual shares of a company. Each share represents a certain percentage of ownership in a company. They are issued by the company and sold at an initial offering and on the secondary market thereafter, wherein investors determine the value of the shares in a bid/ask manner. Shares of stocks provide the holders with certain rights regarding the management of the company, such as voting on new board members. Stocks have historically provided the most return to investors. They are highly recommended for growth in an account, but they are also volatile, and loss of capital is possible. A large allocation of stocks in a portfolio is suitable for a young investor able to take on risk, but it is not suitable for a retiree seeking current income and capital preservation.

INITIAL PUBLIC OFFERING

An **initial public offering**, or **IPO**, describes the initial sale of stock to the public by a company that was formerly privately held. IPOs are usually used by a small or new company pursuing additional capital to expand operations but are also occasionally employed by larger private companies wanting to be publicly traded.

INVOLVED GOVERNMENTAL ORGANIZATION

Any company seeking to offer an IPO must first register with the **Securities and Exchange Commission**, or the **SEC**. There are several steps required to publicly offer a security:

1. The company must submit a **registration statement** to the SEC containing valid information about the issuance of the security, such as the purpose of the issue, public offering price, balance sheet, and so on.
2. The company must then undergo to a twenty-day **cooling-off period** in which the SEC reviews and requires additions or corrections to the registration statement. Twenty days is a minimum; cooling periods can last for many months, while the proper changes are made. During this time, a preliminary or *red herring* prospectus may then be made available to potential buyers of the security who have acknowledged interest. This enables the investor to become familiar with the issue, but it is not yet available for public purchase.
3. After the cooling period ends, the security reaches the **effective date**, and the security is now available for sale. Investors must now be furnished with a final prospectus that summarizes the information in the registration statement in an abbreviated format.

Filing Date and Effective Date for Securities Registration

The **filing date** is the date when the (hopeful) issuer of securities files the requisite registration statement with the SEC. This filing date initiates the cooling-off period, which is at least twenty days long.

The **effective date** is the date when the cooling-off period ends, that is, once the securities are cleared for public sale.

Cooling-off Period and Due Diligence Meetings

Issuers of securities are required to file with the SEC for the new offering. At the date of filing, a **cooling-off period** commences, at the end of which the issue is either cleared or rejected for public sale. The cooling-off period lasts at least twenty days, and during it, underwriters can advertise for the offering and solicit (nonbinding) indications of interest. Syndicate members are permitted to leave the underwriting agreement within the cooling-off period, but forbidden once the period has ended.

Near the end of the cooling-off period, the underwriter holds a meeting to give information for the new offering to syndicate members, selling groups, brokers, institutions, and any other interested parties. This is the **due diligence meeting**, designed to ensure that all material information related to the offering is disclosed to potential investors.

Common Stock

Common stock is an equity security representative of shares of ownership in a company. They are tradable securities that are fairly liquid if there is enough demand for the stock of the company. **Common stockholder**s benefit from ownership by having input on the operation of the company, such as voting rights on membership on the board. Board voting rights are only afforded to common stockholders, not preferred stockholders. Common stock tends to be the most volatile of all securities, with high gains or losses possible intraday. This makes them risky, but historically stocks have provided the highest gains in long-term investing. Common stockholders are the lowest tier to receive compensation for losses in the event of corporate liquidation.

American Depositary Receipts

American depositary receipts, or **ADRs**, are tradable certificates representing shares of stock traded on foreign exchanges. For ADRs to be traded on stock exchanges in the United States, they must be sponsored by a United State bank. To facilitate trade on American exchanges, ADRs use United State dollars as their native denomination. ADRs have several intrinsic benefits of which investors may take advantage. ADRs effectively bypass duties imposed on such transactions and the administrative costs related thereto if the same security had been purchased on a foreign exchange. Additionally, investors benefit by taking part in investing in foreign ventures while receiving gains and dividends in United States currency.

Foreign Stocks

Foreign stocks present many unique opportunities for investors. Foreign stocks give the investor access to growth in emerging markets, which can be very valuable in stagnate domestic markets. Along with unique growth opportunities, unique challenges are also presented. Because foreign stocks are not **registered** with the Securities Exchange Commission, there is a certain lack of transparency as to the company's operation that is not present in domestic stock markets. Foreign stocks are also subject to currency risk due to being value in non-US dollar denominations. Volatility in the country in which the investor invested is also a risk. These risks range from war to sociopolitical issues to regime change. These challenges can be addressed by investing in American depositary receipts, exchange traded funds, and mutual funds.

Preferred Stock

Preferred stock is an equity security representative of shares of ownership in a company. They are tradable securities that are fairly liquid if there is enough demand for the stock of the company. Preferred stocks tend to pay a higher dividend than those received from common stock but do not appreciate as quickly as common stock. Investors seeking current income with exposure to equity growth find this trait appealing. **Preferred stockholders** also must receive their dividends before common stockholders. These dividends are usually (though not always) guaranteed. Preferred stock tends to be less volatile than common stock, and while this results in slower growth, it also lends to less loss in a down market. Preferred stockholders do not have voting rights in a company's decision-making process. If a company were to be liquidated, preferred stockholders receive assets before common stockholders but after unsecured debt holders, making them second from the bottom on the list.

Convertible Preferred Stock

Convertible preferred stock is similar to preferred stock, but it differs in that it may be converted to common stock after a certain time given to the investor at purchase. As the price of preferred stock is usually higher than common stock, a single preferred share will usually convert to multiple **common shares**. If not all of the value of the preferred share is converted to common stock, the remaining value is referred to as the conversion premium. Special risks to consider are the ability of some companies to force conversion when the investor does not desire conversion. Common stock tends to be more volatile than preferred stock and often does not provide the regular dividends inherent to preferred stock. Forced conversion can lead to investment risk when an investor with the goal of current income is forced to find new securities that provide similar and adequate income to replace the income lost by the conversion.

Employee Stock Options

Employee stock options are options to buy a security of a certain company that are given to employees of that company. They are very similar to options bought and sold on major exchanges except that employee stock options are not tradable on exchanges. Employees must usually defer exercising for a set time of vesting. Companies may issue employee stock options as a part of their **retirement savings** or as **taxable bonus compensation**. These retirement incentive plans are tax deferred until redemption. Nonqualified plans are taxable upon receipt instead of redemption.

Restricted Stock

Restricted stock is stock that is held in a company that was not offered as part of an initial public offering. The reason it is considered restricted is because the company and equity issue has not gone through the **vetting process** as required by the Securities Exchange Commission (SEC). While it is not illegal to hold restricted stock, it is illegal to sell it to another investor without taking the proper steps to inform the SEC of the sell and complying with the regulations as stated in section 1244 of the Internal Revenue Code.

Characteristics of Equity Securities

Shareholder Rights

The rights of the shareholders vary between common and preferred stock:

1. **Voting rights**—Common stockholders are afforded voting rights in the operation of the company, especially in the election of board members. Preferred stockholders do not receive the right to vote in matters of operation.
2. **Dividends**—Dividends are the distribution of a portion of a company's earnings to shareholders. Shareholders may receive any dividend declared, but preferred stockholders must be provided with the dividend to which they are entitled before a common stockholder may receive a dividend. Owners of common stock are eligible to receive a dividend distribution if they own the shares before the ex-dividend date (date on or after which new shareholders are no longer entitled to a declared dividend).
3. **Liquidation preference**—In the event of corporate liquidation, stockholders are entitled to receive the residual value in a company after the debtors have been paid. Preferred stock holders will be compensated prior to common stock holders.
4. **Antidilution rights**—Antidilution rights are rights by which investors may prevent the value of their holdings from being diluted from the new issue of stock they are holding. Antidilution rights guarantee the investor the right to purchase enough stock to maintain their current ownership in the company.

Resale Restrictions on Equity Securities

Equity securities can have different restrictions on their resale or transference which then classify the securities as **restricted stock** (also called **Section 1244 stock** or **letter stock**). These restrictions especially apply to executives or other insider employees of a company who would receive stock as compensation but who would not be able to sell the stock given the harms such early selling could bring to the company's stock value. Accordingly, restricted stock can often be on a vesting schedule, such that an employee would fail to retain the stock if he departed from the company before it was fully vested. Resale restrictions on stocks are regulated by the SEC and not merely by private agreements between publicly-traded companies and their insider employees.

Dividend Discount Model and Dividend Payout Ratio

The **dividend discount model** is one that values the price of a particular stock by using the expected future dividends and discounting them back to find the present value. An investor would use the result to determine whether the stock is under or overvalued. Here is the formula:

$$\frac{dividend\ per\ share}{discount\ rate - dividend\ growth\ rate}$$

The **dividend payout ratio** is a percentage measuring the earnings paid to shareholders in the form of dividends. Here is the formula:

$$\frac{yearly\ dividend\ per\ share}{earnings\ per\ share}$$

Methods used to Determine the Value of Equity Securities

Quantitative Methods

Quantitative methods are methods used to better understand a company's or sector's behavior. These methods consist of intricate mathematical and statistical modeling. It can be used to measure performance of a company based on several factors or in the valuation of a firm based on those or other factors. Quantitative methods are also known as **technical analysis**. Technical and quantitative analysis take on many forms, from abstract mathematical formulas to seeking trends in charts and comparing them with similar charts from other securities. As with all other methods of valuation, quantitative methods are a useful tool but should be only part of the picture an investor uses to make an informed decision.

Fundamental Analysis

Fundamental analysis is the method by which investors determine the value of equity securities using data gathered from the company's financial statements. Information from the income statement, the balance sheet, and the statement of cash flows are analyzed to provide a clear picture of the company's profitability, liquidity, and debt management. These fundamental numbers are assessed, and if they are found to be favorable, an investor will place a high valuation on the security, perhaps higher than the current market value. This indicates to the investor that it is a good time to buy the stock. Examples of fundamental analysis include the **price-to-earnings ratio**, or P/E ratio, and **earnings per share**, or EPS.

Fundamental and Technical Analysis

Fundamental and technical analyses are two methods that encourage the observation of trends when making investment decisions. **Fundamental analysis** focuses on the historical performance of the issuing company. It takes into consideration the various financial records of a company in order to predict stock movement. Financial analysis uses balance sheets, income statements and various ratios to determine how a stock will perform. **Technical analysis** requires the study of the company's stock rather than the company's financial history. Technical analysts study the historical performance of a stock's price and then create charts. The charts provide a visual pattern that can be observed by analysts who can interpret the patterns to reveal how a stock will perform.

Types of Pooled Investments

Pooled Investments

Pooled investments, such as unit investment trusts (UITs) and mutual funds, are funds to which more than one investor contributes funds for the purpose of holding them as a **group**. This is done so each of the investors may have access to benefits to which they may not have had access individually. Pooled investments also create economies of scale which in turn lower an individual's administrative costs (such as trading costs) and allow for greater diversification and benefit from professional money managers. Pooled investments also spread the risk over the pool of investors. The major drawback to pooled investments is related to the large pool of investors in regard to capital gains. The capital gains earned on the pooled funds are spread evenly over the pool, regardless of the tenure of the participant.

Open-Ended Investment Companies

Open-ended investment companies are **exchange traded funds companies** that create investments based on their stated objective (usually a basket of stocks, commodities, bonds, or some combination thereof) and issues an unlimited number of shares to be purchased. The new money received from investors is invested in the company's fund across the spectrum of their chosen investments. The investor may then redeem those shares for the fund's net asset value. Redemption is accomplished via the company purchasing shares back from the client. **Mutual funds** are the most common type of open-ended investment company. For a low initial outlay of capital, investors have exposure to commodities, bonds, and stocks and benefit from diversification inherent to the fund.

Closed-Ended Investment Companies

Closed-ended investment companies are companies that are formed for the purpose of issuing a stock based on a basket of **underlying assets**. These assets consist of stocks, bonds, commodities, real estate, and any asset that can be securitized. After determining the amount of capital they need to raise, closed-ended investment companies must then submit their fund to the public through an initial public offering and all registrations required by the Securities Exchange Commission for an initial public offering. Unlike open-ended funds, there are a finite number of shares in a closed-ended investment company fund. They are traded like stocks on exchanges and valued similarly to stocks. The most common form of closed-ended funds are **exchange trade funds**, or ETFs.

SAI

All information that an investment company is required to provide to investors before they purchase shares in the company is provided in the prospectus. However, some investors and members of the public may desire additional information about the company beyond what's provided in the prospectus. This additional information, such as the history of the company, or a detailed financial profile, are in the **statement of additional information (SAI)**, and must be provided to potential investors upon request. These days, the SAI is commonly provided on the company website.

Registration Statement

When an investment company files a registration statement with the SEC, it consists of two parts. The first part is the **prospectus**. This is the information that every potential investor in the company must be provided with before they're allowed to purchase the company's shares. The prospectus is also known as a summary prospectus, or an NI-A prospectus. The second part is the **information** that must be on file with the SEC and available for public inspection, but is not required to be provided to all potential investors. It is also called the statement of additional information (SAI).

Hedge Funds

Hedge funds are alternative investments that seek high returns through the use of **sophisticated investment management strategies**. They tend to be very aggressively managed and use some combination of leverage, long/short strategies, and derivative contracts to generate the highest returns possible. This strategy also leads to higher-than-normal risk, and limits their investor pool to high-net-worth individuals and institutional investors. Since those who invest in hedge funds are typically sophisticated and experienced investors, there is little regulation of hedge funds. High minimum investments also limit their investors to higher-net-worth individuals as well. Contrary to their moniker, hedge funds are generally not used to hedge risk, but to maximize returns. Hedge funds are not generally open to retail investors and lack liquidity due to minimum time commitments of the investors' capital.

Characteristics of Hedge Funds

Hedge funds are similar in structure to mutual funds, but they are dissimilar in that they are **unregulated** (because private) and thus have a wider array of investment options. Hedge funds are characteristically very **risky and speculative**, using purchases on margin, short sales, and other higher-risk investment strategies to aggressively make a profit.

Hedge funds' riskiness seems to contradict their name, since hedging is the reduction of risk—but the reason for the name is that, when hedge funds historically arose, one of their main purposes was to hedge against the risk of a bear market by selling short.

Hedge funds have very limited liquidity, often keeping investors' money for at least one year.

For tax purposes, hedge funds will be arranged as limited partnerships, so that they will qualify as flow-through entities. The manager of the fund (or an affiliate) will be the general partner, and the investors will be limited partners.

Private Equity

Private equity consists of any equity which isn't quoted on any public exchanges. **Private investments** might involve funding a private company to develop new technologies, or simply to be more successful in general. Private equity also might involve purchasing a public company for the sake of making it private. Private equity often involves investors with enormous amounts of capital.

Accredited Investor and Venture Capital

An **accredited investor** is an individual who makes at least $200,000 per year (or $300,000 with a spouse) or has a net worth of at least $1 million.

Venture capital is the money provided by investors to help start-up firms. This is a way for small businesses that do not have access to the capital markets to get the money they need without utilizing bank loans as their sole source of funding.

Usefulness of Hedge Funds to Investors

Hedge funds are pooled investments used by wealthy individuals to take advantage of risky alternative investments that are not allowed by law in mutual funds. Such alternative investments take the form of short selling, swaps, derivatives, buying and selling on margin, and arbitrage. Hedge funds are able to accomplish this due to their **exemption** from government laws and regulations pertaining to mutual funds. The maximum number of investors per hedge fund is 100, which often results in very high minimum investments. Hedge funds charge management fees, as do mutual funds, but they also collect a percentage of the profits, usually about 20 percent%.

Unit Investments Trusts

Unit investment trusts (UITs) are pooled investments. UITs are created when investment companies that are registered with the Securities Exchange Commission buy a portfolio of **income-producing securities** and sell participation in the portfolio to investors in the forms of shares of the trust. UITs are characterized by their lack of management and lower fees than other similar investments. The portfolio remains fixed for the life of the trust. Interest payments, dividends, and capital gains are regularly distributed to the shareholders. UITs are generally considered low-risk investments and suitable for investors seeking current income and capital preservation. They would not be suitable for someone seeking growth in a portfolio.

ETFs

Exchange traded funds, or ETFs, are securities that are traded like individual securities but are made up of multiple securities or a commodity or are designed to mirror the performance of an index. ETFs are similar to open-ended mutual funds in that a single share is made up of multiple assets. Unlike open-ended mutual funds, however, ETFs are not valued at net asset value because it trades like a stock. Expense ratios and fees also tend to be lower on ETFs than those of open-ended mutual funds. ETFs can also be used to give investors access to commodities at lower costs and initial investment than purchasing actual commodities.

REITs

Real estate investment trusts, or REITs, are a type of pooled investment that invests the investors' funds in income property (rental units), or equity REITs, and mortgage loans, or mortgage REITs. REITs trade on exchanges similarly to stocks. REITs provide investors with access to the real estate markets while remaining liquid, which is uncharacteristic of real estate investing. Investors also have access to investing in commercial property through REITs as well, where the capital requirement to invest in commercial real estate may have been previously prohibitive. REITs also provide income in the form of dividends while making capital appreciation possible through the real estate market.

Characteristics of Pooled Investments

Methods to Determine the Value of Pooled Investments

Net asset value, sometimes referred to **NAV**, refers to the value of all underlying assets minus liabilities divided by outstanding shares. This is the most common valuation of mutual fund shares and usually the price point at which they trade. Exchange traded funds have a NAV because they are pooled investments based on a group of holdings, but they do not trade at that NAV. Because exchange traded funds trade on exchanges similarly to stocks, they are valued based on supply, demand, and NAV. Supply and demand may make that price higher than NAV (traded at a premium) or lower than NAV (traded at a discount).

Types of Derivative Securities

Options

Options contracts are contracts between two or more investors based on the right or requirement to buy or sell a certain security that underlies the contract. The most basic types of options are **calls** and **puts**. More advanced options contracts are some combination of the two surrounding a strike price. Options are used for many reasons. A **covered call** can produce risk-free income for a retiree, whereas an investor who wishes to speculate on the price of an investment may purchase a **straddle**. The retiree selling the covered call receives the premium paid for the call and experiences no risk associated with the income because he or she owns the underlying security. The value of a straddle is realized when the price of the security experiences large amounts of volatility in either direction.

Warrants

Warrants are derivative securities that allow the investor to buy securities directly from the issuer at a given price within a defined period of time. Warrants are usually included at no additional charge with a new issue of debt instruments to entice investors to buy the investment. In this case, warrants are referred to as **sweeteners**. Warrants differ from call options in that they originate from the issuing company, and calls are sold by other investors. Warrants also tend to have longer periods until expiration than options, usually measured in years instead of the months common to options. Investors benefit from warrants in several ways. They can sell them to other investors and collect the premium for a security in which they had no investment, or they can exercise them and buy a well-performing security for less than market value.

Forward Contract and Futures Contract

Two general categories of contracts exist in futures trading. They are forward (or cash) contract, and futures contracts. Both are legally binding agreements to buy or sell some commodity or financial instrument in the future. However, **forward contracts** are not standardized. They are privately negotiated contracts between buyer and seller.

Futures contracts are standardized in terms of quality, quantity, delivery time, and location. Futures contracts have the obvious benefit in that they are more liquid because they are standardized.

Liquidity of a commodity is a characteristic that allows large transactions to occur without a significant impact on the price of that commodity. This is possible due to the high quantity of units of the particular commodity. Institutional traders prefer liquid investments to help minimize market fluctuations due to their own trading activities.

Derivative Securities

Derivative securities are those securities that derive their existence based on other securities. Without the existence of the underlying security, derivatives would not exist. Derivatives are created when an investor or group of investors make securities based on other securities available to other investors. These derivatives range from the ultra-risky and speculative to the ultrasafe, income-producing derivatives. Examples of derivatives include options, futures, and forward contracts, among others. **Speculative derivatives** are complex securities that investors purchase in hopes of capital appreciation but at great risk. **Income-producing derivatives** often take the form of selling covered call options, which provides no risk of loss and provides current income to the selling investor.

The most common derivative securities are the following:

1. **Options**—Options are tradable contracts that provide the purchaser with the right to buy or sell the underlying security at certain price, or strike price, within a specified time frame.
2. **Futures**—Futures are contracts that require the buyer to buy (or seller to sell) a specific asset at a set date in the future at a set price. The quality and volume of the asset will also be predetermined.
3. **Forward contracts**—Forward contracts are similar to futures in that they are contracts between buyers and sellers to buy or sell an asset at a future date, but unlike futures contracts, forward contracts are a cash transaction with the delivery of the asset taking place in the future.

Alternative Investments

Alternative investments, or **alts**, are investments that are considered to be nontraditional investments, with traditional investments considered to be stocks, bonds, and cash. Alts include but are not limited to commodities, options and other derivatives, and real estate. These assets provide exposure to investments that are not correlated to the stock or bond market, thus providing a hedge against volatility. Alts are useful to investors who are seeking exposure to assets other than stocks and bonds to diversify their portfolios and provide uncorrelated assets in the event of market decline or recession.

Limited Partnerships

Limited partnerships are a form of alternative investment in which an investor may take part in the business venture on a limited basis. To this end, he or she is only **liable** for the business to the extent of the investment, but he or she participates in the partnership's **profits**. If he or she loses the full investment, he or she is no longer liable for the company's debts. Investors find limited partnerships attractive because the partnerships provide them with access to nontraditional investments, such as business ventures, without exposing them to personal risk of liability if a company becomes insolvent. The amount of loss possible is the same as possible in regards to traditional investments: only the amount invested.

ETNs

Exchange-traded notes (ETNs) are hybrid securities which serve as a mixture of bonds and exchange-traded funds (ETFs). As their name implies, they are traded on an exchange, although they also have a maturity date like bonds. But with ETNs, the repayment of principal at the maturity date is modified according to the day's market index factor. (Further, the repayment is reduced by investing fees.) The value of an ETN, however, is not simply based on the market index, but also depends on the creditworthiness of the debtor company, since ETNs are unsecured debt instruments.

Unlike ordinary bonds, ETNs do not have periodic coupon payments.

Leveraged Funds, Inverse Funds, and Viatical Settlements

Leveraged funds (also called leveraged exchange-traded funds, or leveraged ETFs) use leverage in the form of debt or derivative securities, such as futures or options contracts, to try to intensify the return of a given stock index. Thus a leveraged ETF based on the S&P 500 index might aim to provide a 2-to-1 return on that index, with any rise or fall in the index being doubled in the investor's portfolio due to the leverage involved in his investment.

Inverse funds (also called inverse ETFs) are meant to follow the opposite trajectory of the index (or other package of securities) to which they correspond. While an ETF might ordinarily track directly with the S&P 500, for instance, an inverse ETF aims to track conversely with it, increasing as the S&P 500 decreases and vice versa. This inverse relationship is established through derivative contracts like futures and options.

Viatical settlements (also called life settlements) involve the owner of a life insurance contract—usually the same person insured by the contract—selling this contract at a discount in order to receive some of the death benefit in advance. This would probably be done in the event of terminal and costly illness. Hence an owner of a $1,000,000 life insurance policy, if he contracted cancer, might sell his policy for $900,000 to a third party.

Structured Products

Structured products are securities which are linked to some other underlying asset, such as another security, a group of securities, a commodity, and index, or something else.

Structured products can sometimes have a **"principal guarantee" feature**, which means simply that the principal is guaranteed to return if the investor holds the investment for long enough (e.g., to maturity for debt securities).

Insurance Based Products

Variable Annuities

Variable annuities are life insurance products that provide investors a stream of income. These payments **vary** (hence variable annuity) based on the performance of the underlying security.

Investors typically don't start taking their income stream until retirement and are in need of income. Variable annuities are attractive to investors because it is possible to achieve a higher income with variable annuities than with fixed annuities if the underlying assets perform well. Contract riders are available with variable annuities that guarantee a minimum payment based upon a locked-in (or stepped-up) contract value. Variable annuities are usually only suitable for retirees or someone who is close to retirement. Variable annuities also tend to have high fees and large up-front commissions paid to the broker. This can affect account performance and tempts brokers to sell unsuitable investments.

Fixed Annuities

Fixed annuities are life insurance products that provide a guaranteed stream of income to the holder, or **annuitant**, for the totality of the period specified in the contract. Depending upon the contract, this may be a defined period or remainder of the life of the annuitant. Fixed annuities are attractive to investors because the payments provided are **guaranteed** and do not fluctuate based on the performance of the initial investment. In this way, the insurance company bears all the investment risk of a fixed annuity, and the investor bears none. Fixed annuities often occupy a portion of the fixed income sector of portfolio allocation. The attractiveness of each annuity varies accordingly with the amount of payment guaranteed.

Indexed Annuities

Equity indexed annuities are life insurance products that provide a stream of income for the life of the annuity contract, whose underlying account performance is indexed to **equity markets**, such as the Dow Jones Industrial Average and the Standard and Poor's 500. While the initial investment of capital is shielded from loss due to the annuity product, it may experience gains in conjunction with the performance of equity market to which it is linked. Equity indexed annuities are useful to investors who are risk averse but still seek capital appreciation for retirement income. While the upside sounds attractive, the returns are often limited by insurance carrier-imposed caps and further reduced by annual fees associated with the account.

Life Insurance

Life insurance is an insurance product underwritten by licensed companies to help investors protect against the loss of income resulting from the **death of the insured person**. Life insurance helps investors plan for unforeseen or early death by providing income to the survivors of the deceased to replace the income lost by the loss of life. Life insurance can be useful in paying for funeral expenses, unpaid debt against large assets such as a house, and future expenses such college tuition for children. The types of life insurance available to investors are **whole** life insurance, **term** life insurance, **universal** life insurance, and **variable** life insurance.

Whole Life Insurance

Whole life insurance is a life insurance policy purchased with regular, fixed premiums that covers the **entire**, or whole, life of the insured rather than a specific time period, as is the case with term life insurance. Unlike term life insurance, whole life insurance can accrue a cash value over the life of the policy. The premiums paid into the whole life plan cover the costs related with insurance and accumulates equity in a savings account. The face value of the policy is paid to the beneficiary at death, but not the savings account. The balance of the savings account is usually invested in fixed-income securities and suffers from interest rate and inflation risk. This prevents whole life insurance from becoming a viable capital appreciation investment.

Term Life Insurance

Term life insurance is a life insurance policy purchased with regular, fixed premiums that covers the life of an individual for a **term** specified in the insurance contract. If the insured person dies during the specified term, the face value of the policy is paid to the insured's beneficiary. Unlike whole life insurance, however, term life insurance does not accrue a cash value. After the term life insurance has expired, the insurance company retains all premiums paid, and there is no longer a benefit to the insured. Term life insurance policies are often attractive to young investors because of the low monthly premiums and ease of access to term life policies as they are often offered through the investor's employer. Term policies can help provide the deceased's beneficiary with funds for funeral expenses and other immediate needs arising after the death of the insured.

Universal Life Insurance

Universal life insurance is a life insurance policy purchased with variable premiums that covers the life of the insured for its **entirety** rather than for a stated fixed term. Universal life insurance is similar to whole life insurance in that it covers the insured for his or her entire life and can accrue a cash value. Unlike whole life insurance, variable life allows the investor to assign to which account the premium goes. If the investor would rather increase coverage, he or she may assign it to the insurance account. If the investor would rather the cash value grow, he or she may assign it to the internal savings account. These products tend to be attractive to investors who desire greater control over their money but still seek life insurance coverage for the length of their remaining life.

Variable Life Insurance

Variable life insurance is a life insurance policy purchased with fixed premiums that covers the **entire life** of the insured. Variable life insurance policies are invested in stock and bond markets to facilitate account appreciation. The appreciated amount may then be used to purchase more insurance or pay the premiums, which could lower the amount of investment required of the investor. If the account depreciates, however, the investor may be forced to pay more to meet the premium or risk losing the insurance. Poor account performance can also lead to a decrease in coverage. The nature of variable life insurance policies being tied to the stock market tends to make them higher-fee policies and requires the selling broker to be licensed with Financial Industry Regulatory Authority (FINRA).

Other Assets

Investment Real Estate and Characteristics

Investment real estate involves any real estate—buildings, fixtures, land, and associated natural resources—held for the purpose of **profit** rather than **residence**. This profit can arise either from recurring income, such as lease or rental income, or from unrealized appreciation in value. Oftentimes even properties held for the purpose of producing income are also held to grow in value and so provide a capital gain on sale. Given all the issues involved in dealing with tenants, investment real estate held for the purpose of residential rental income can be very time- and labor-intensive, unless one wishes to outsource such work to an outside property manager.

Investment Characteristics of Commodities and Precious Metals

Commodities are basic goods extracted from **natural resources** with minimal processing. These can include animal flesh like beef or pork; crops like wheat, rice, or beans; raw materials like iron ore, natural gas, or lumber; and precious metals like gold, silver, or platinum. Because of their minimal processing, commodities are broadly interchangeable no matter the producer providing them on the market, and thus demand the same price even if some producers' commodities might vary slightly in value compared to others. Commodities are frequently traded through futures contracts and on regulated exchanges.

Precious metals are metals with a high economic value, not infrequently due to their rarity. They are generally traded either through futures contracts or in terms of the physical assets themselves, such as coins or bars. Precious metals, like commodities in general, can also be traded in terms of mutual funds and exchange-traded funds.

Investment Vehicle Characteristics Chapter Quiz

1. Which of the following is not considered a money market security?

a. Treasury Bill
b. Jumbo negotiable certificates of deposit
c. 14-month commercial paper
d. 1-month variable rate demand obligations

2. Using the Rule of 72, which of the following investments would double in 14 years?

a. A preferred stock paying 6%
b. A corporate bond paying 7%
c. A municipal bond paying 5%
d. A common stock paying 2% dividend and growing by 5%

3. An investor in a 30% marginal federal tax bracket and a 7% state tax bracket would be better off buying:

a. A corporate bond yielding 5.2%
b. An out-of-state municipal bond yielding 4%
c. A Puerto Rico municipal bond yielding 3.5%
d. A US Treasury bond yielding 4.2%

4. A bond rating from Moody's of Baa is equal to:

a. S&P AA
b. Fitch's BBB
c. S&P A
d. Fitch's BB

5. Which of the following has the most exposure to liquidation priority?

a. Common stockholders
b. Preferred stockholders
c. Bondholders
d. Lien holders

6. The difference in yields between the 10-yr Treasury and high yield "junk" bonds is the yield spread, also called the "risk premium". When the spread widens, it is an indicator of which of the following?

1. Investor confidence in the economy
2. Investor fears for the economy
3. Investor preference for stocks over bonds
4. Investor preference for safer investments

a. 1 and 3
b. 2 and 4
c. 1 and 4
d. 2 and 3

7. Which is not a benefit of investing in Preferred stock over common stock?

a. Senior position in a liquidation event
b. Senior position in dividend payments
c. Greater chance for capital gains
d. Don't have to bother with voting rights issues

8. One primary advantage of reinvesting mutual fund dividends is:

a. Dividends are not taxed when reinvested
b. The sales charge is reduced
c. Additional shares are purchased at NAV
d. There is no advantage

9. An investor sells 1,000 shares of stock that he's held for two years for $11,500. He has received dividends of $200 over that time and his capital gain is $2,500, what is his cost basis?

a. $8,800
b. $9,000
c. $9,200
d. $9.00

10. Which of the following is not true of both Exchange Traded Funds and Unit Investment Trusts?

a. Diversification
b. Passive management
c. Instant liquidity
d. Niche investing opportunities

Investment Vehicle Characteristics Chapter Quiz Answers

1. C: Money market securities are 12 months or less, with the majority maturing in six months or less. Usually they are issued at a discount.

2. C: A municipal bond paying 5% would double in approximately 14 years. 72 divided by 5 = 14.4.

3. B: Corporate bonds are not tax-exempt, out-of-state muni bonds are exempt from federal income taxes but usually not state income taxes, Puerto Rico muni bonds are exempt from all levels of income tax, and US Treasury bonds are exempt solely from federal income tax. Hence the corporate bond's TEY is 5.2%, the out-of-state bond's TEY = 4% / (1 – 30%) = 5.71%, the Puerto Rico bond's TEY = 3.5% / (1 – 30% - 7%) = 5.56%, and the Treasury bond's TEY = 4.2% / (1 – 7%) = 4.52%. The out-of-state bond has the highest tax-equivalent yield (TEY).

Puerto Rico bonds are local, state, and federal tax free. The TEY is 5.55% better than the other alternatives after taxation is considered.

4. B: Fitch's, and S&P's, BBB rating is equivalent to Moody's Baa.

5. A: Common stockholders are at the end of the line in a liquidation scenario, often receiving nothing at all after more senior parties are paid.

6. B: When the risk premium widens, it implies that investors are risk averse. Usually in response to concerns for economic growth. When this happens, safer bonds are purchased and yields on riskier bonds need to be higher to attract investors.

7. C: Common stocks are much more likely to have capital gains than preferreds. Preferred stock doesn't have voting rights.

8. C: While you may pay a 5.5% sales charge on a mutual fund investment, when dividends are reinvested in additional shares, they are bought at NAV.

9. B: $9,000 is his cost basis. 9,000 plus 2,500 is 11,500. In this case, the number of shares or share price is irrelevant, and the dividends were not reinvested so they don't impact the cost basis but were taxed as income when received.

10. C: ETFs are traded just like a stock and have constant and instant liquidity, whereas UITs do not.

Client Investment Recommendations and Strategies

Type of Client

Individual

An **individual** is a singular person that invests for him- or herself. An individual is usually a natural person and not a corporation. Individuals are typically referred to as **small investors** or as **retail investors**. The reference to retail investing refers to the fact that they are not large, institutional investors. Often, individual investors are unable to access certain types of investments that may have large minimum buy-ins. The sophistication of each individual varies from person to person depending upon life experience, but the level of sophistication is usually significantly less than that of institutional investors.

Sole Proprietorship

Sole proprietorships are business structures that investors may use to their advantage concerning simplicity for purposes of **taxation**. A business that is formed by the owner and not structured as a limited liability corporation, but a sole proprietorship, may report its income and losses on the individual owner's income tax returns. This may lead to some tax advantages, such as reduced reportable income for the individual, but it also makes the owner (sole proprietor) liable for all of the business' debts. In this case, a failed venture on the part of the investor would not limit the investor's loss to the investment in the venture but gives creditors access to the client's personal assets as well.

Business Entities Considered Clients

General partnership—business venture in which two or more partners accept liability for debts accepted by the business. General partnerships do not limit the liability of the partners involved, and personal assets are at stake.

Limited partnership—business venture in which general partners manage the business and assume liability for the company's debt, but limited partners are only liable up to the amount of their investment. Limited partners also participate in any earnings made.

Limited liability company—business venture in which the owners are limited in their liability regarding the company's debt. This is done without requiring incorporation.

C-Corporation—business structure by which the company itself is made into a legal person and assumes all legal and financial liabilities. The revenues of a C-Corp are taxed to the corporation.

S-Corporation—business structure by which the company itself is made into a legal person and assumes all legal and financial liabilities. S-Corps must be composed of no more than 100 investors. The revenues of S-Corps are passed through to the investors and are not taxed at the corporate level.

Trusts and Estates

Trusts and are estates are means by which investors protect their money from several different factors. **Estates** are the property left behind by a deceased person. If the deceased did not leave explicit instructions concerning their wishes for the disposition of their assets, a probate court will be required to assign those assets' disposition. This often leads to nonpositive results for the decedent's assets and the heirs to whom the decedent wished their assets be passed. **Trusts** are legal arrangements by which investors may protect their assets. They are vetted as legal and valid before the decedent's death to avoid probate court and the unnecessary loss of assets. Trust documents assign a trustee to carry out the deceased's wishes in accordance with the trust documents and make the passing of wealth and assets an easier transition.

Foundations and Charities as Possible Investment Clients

Even though **foundations and charities**, as well as other nonprofit organizations, are not seeking to maximize profit as a central organizational aim, they may yet utilize **investments** for the sake of their funding and growth. Foundations and charities, to the extent that they do not rely on donors, may even depend upon **investment returns** as crucial to their ongoing activity. This is especially true for foundations. Alternatively, foundations and charities may wish to supplement significant donations with investment returns anyway. In any case, the role of investments to foundations and charities requires an investment adviser to consider how his services could provide value to such nonprofit organizations.

Client Profile

Client's Investment Profile

A **client's investment profile** is a multifaceted look at the client's **current situation and goals**. It consists of many factors to be considered. The advisor must be aware of the client's current income, their goals regarding retirement, their plans regarding their eventual death and possible disability, and their time horizon and risk tolerance. It is also important to consider their current financial status including their cash flows, their balance sheet of assets, any existing investments, and their tax situation. Lastly, and just as important, are the nonfinancial investment considerations including their values, attitude, experience and level of sophistication, and their demographics. Each of the preceding factors plays an important part in determining the client's investment profile. None of them, however, should be taken individually to determine the entire profile as some of the investor's needs can't be met in this situation.

Meeting a Client's Current Income Needs

A major part of the client's investment profile is current income and the **need for current income**. For an investor that has not yet reached retirement, his or her needs may be being met by his or her occupation. If those needs are not being met, or if the client is in retirement, there are several strategies by which an advisor may help the client meet this need. If an investor has a longer time horizon but still desires capital appreciation and income, there are several options available. Large companies often pay regular dividends on shares of their common stock. This allows for current income and capital appreciation through the stock markets. Preferred stocks also regularly pay dividends and tend to appreciate more than bonds. For an investor concerned with capital preservation and income, bonds provide a relatively safe investment with regular interest payments made to the investor.

Managing Cash Flow

Cash flows are a very important part of the client's investment profile. The client's need for cash should be regularly discussed to ensure that current needs are being met and future needs will be met. This discussion takes many forms, whether it is advising a client against a specific investment because it will be illiquid and tie up funds that are needed for regular expenses or advising a client to invest in income-paying investments to ensure future cash flows. Ensuring **present and future cash flows** should be considered with every decision the client makes as it is part of the fiduciary responsibility of the advisor.

Evaluating a Client's Balance Sheet

The **client's balance sheet** is very important in determining the client's investment profile. That balance sheet is a summary of the client's **net worth** as related to their assets and liabilities. From the balance sheet, the advisor can determine the **solvency** of the investor and make a suitable judgment as to their needs involving investing and financial planning. This statement of the investor's condition is helpful when discussing suggestions and advice given to the client. If the client is doubtful about advice given or reluctant to make a change in financial habits, the balance sheet is often the easiest way to show the client why the advice was given and that it is in the best interest of the client.

Knowledge of Client's Existing Investments

It is important to know every facet of the client's **financial status**. In knowing a client's existing holdings, an advisor is better equipped to make sound financial suggestions. Awareness of the client's **existing investments** is key to making informed suggestions to the client. If the client's current holdings are suitable to the client's needs, then the advisor need not acquire those holdings again. If they are not suitable to the client's needs, then the advisor should inform the client thereof. There are also special financial benefits for the investor, should the advisor know the quantity and types of existing investments. Certain investments, such as mutual funds, provide investors with discounts known as break points when the investor reaches certain levels of investment.

Understanding a Client's Tax Situation

Taxation situations vary from client to client, as do the needs of each client. Rarely will an advisor ever have two clients with identical taxation situations. Knowing the client's tax situation is vital to making **suitable recommendations** to the client. Investors investing in tax-deferred retirement accounts do not need to be worried about tax implications from capital gains or interest received in the deferred account. If the same investor also invests in nonqualified taxable investment accounts, those same capital gains and interests paid become issues. Knowing which types of investments are tax advantaged and which are not becomes very important in this case. Alternatively, knowing a client's adjusted gross income and their respective tax brackets also help the advisor make informed suggestions. A client on the cusp of a new tax bracket may be bumped into a new bracket and adversely affected if the advisor recommends selling a position with a large capital gain. Conversely, the investor would benefit from the losses from the sale of a toxic asset and the effect it may have on the investor's adjusted gross income.

Helping Clients Meet Capital Goals in a Specific Time Frame

When determining clients' financial goals, it is important to assist them in achieving **all of their objectives**, not just the ones the advisor may consider most important. These goals may have a long time horizon, such as retirement, or a shorter time horizon, such as saving for a child's education. These goals should be considered when advising on **proper asset allocation**. Bonds may not be the best investment for a young worker who is saving for retirement, as they provide little growth, but if that same worker is saving for his children's college tuition or to buy a house, bonds may be the appropriate investment vehicle. While bonds do not provide the growth (capital appreciation) needed to fund retirement, they may provide the stability of capital needed when saving for a short-term goal.

CLIENT'S RISK TOLERANCE

Many factors are to be considered when defining a **client's risk tolerance**. Time horizon is a very important factor. If an investor is unsure of their **need for risk**, their time horizon may be a very helpful and informative metric. For clients with a long horizon, more aggressive and risky investments may be the solution to the need of capital appreciation. For clients with shorter time horizons, safer and less-volatile investments may be more in line with their risk tolerance. Time horizon, however, should not be the only factor of risk tolerance considered. Investor personality is also a large factor when determining risk tolerance. An investor with a long time horizon may have no stomach for volatility and loss and may therefore be better suited to less-aggressive and safer investments.

NONFINANCIAL INVESTMENT CONSIDERATIONS

All investors have unique life experiences that shape their desires and wants in investing. Considering this, not all investors seek maximum return for their outlay of capital. Many investors consider their **values** when investing and prefer not to invest in companies that are not in line with their values. This may include companies such as tobacco and firearms companies. This same consideration, however, may lead them to desire to invest in other companies that, while they are in line with the investor's values, may not provide the most benefit. A client's attitude toward current world events and political environments may also affect their investment decisions. Clients' investing experience and sophistication vary widely, and the advisor should be aware of both facts and advise accordingly. **Investor demographics** vary as widely as any other nonfinancial aspect of the investor's profile. Demographics can determine an investor's need for life and disability insurance; the investment time horizon, sophistication, and many other factors should be considered when making informed investment advice.

LIFE INSURANCE AND ESTATE PLANNING

Clients can help prepare for eventual death by purchasing life insurance and participating in estate planning. **Life insurance policies** can help the deceased's beneficiaries cope with the loss of income caused by the death of the insured. Life insurance proceeds are helpful with many expenses including but not limited to the deceased's funeral, college tuition for the deceased's children, and helping a spouse pay off a mortgage. **Estate planning** is also important for the client to consider. While life insurance helps meet the financial needs of the beneficiaries, estate planning helps ensure that the deceased's wishes are fulfilled with minimal loss of assets due to taxation and legal fees.

PLANNING FOR DISABILITY

Many investors at some point in life experience some level of **disability**. This can result in loss of income for the investor, which can then endanger assets that guarantee financial liabilities. To help a client plan for this possibility, advisors should be familiar with disability insurance. **Disability insurance** is an insurance policy that helps the insured cope with the loss of income resulting from disability by providing payments to the injured party, usually for a specific period of time. Needs for disability insurance vary from client to client. The main and most obvious need for compensation is replacement of current income. A client with a high income will require a higher disability income. Also of consideration is the client's occupation. A client in a sedentary job who works from home may not experience much loss of income from injury if they are able to continue working despite injury, whereas a person on a construction crew may not be able to produce income at all.

Forming a Specific Investment Strategy by Gathering Client Data

Because investment strategies and portfolios aim not merely to maximize returns but to meet a particular client's cash-flow objectives and fulfill various social objectives of his, it is important for an investment advisor to **gather client data** in crafting his particular **investment strategy**. This data gathering can take the form of questionnaires and interviews to learn relevant facts which the client is best able to answer, as well as other demographic research to learn relevant facts of which the client may be less aware. In doing these, it is important for the investment advisor to gain relevant data while also not infringing upon the client's sense of privacy.

Client's Time Horizon

Each client is considered to have a **time horizon**, or period of time in which their **assets** are to be invested. Advisors should always know a client's time horizon as it is critical to help the client make the most informed and suitable decisions and investments regarding their funds. Time horizons may contain **significant events** such as college attendance for the investors' children, the marriage of an investor's child, retirement, and eventually the death of the client. Understanding when the investor expects to experience these significant events is necessary to provide suitable investment advice. The time horizon is what helps advisors know if they should recommend aggressive investments (for someone with a **longer time horizon**) or more conservative investments (for someone with a **short time horizon**).

A client's **time horizon** is one of the most critical aspects of a client's investment profile. The time horizon helps the advisor, and in many cases the investor, understand the length of time the investor needs money and how to ensure it will last the length of the entire time horizon. A client that desires a high level of spending in retirement and has a short time horizon to retirement may require more aggressive investments than normal to help reach that goal. Alternatively, if a client is happy with the current level of spending and does not wish for increases in lifestyle spending, less aggressive investing is appropriate to preserve the capital from which the current income flows.

Capital Market Theory

CAPM

The **Capital Asset Pricing Model**, or **CAPM**, is a model used to value securities by comparing the relative risk of the asset to the expected return of the asset. CAPM is based on the risk/reward theory that an investor should expect greater return if the investor takes greater risk. The metric target that applies to the *greater* wording of the CAPM is the expected return of risk-free securities, usually United States Treasuries. CAPM is very useful to investors that would like to know if their investment is worth the capital outlay versus the opportunity of not investing in another security.

Modern Portfolio Theory

Modern portfolio theory attempts to provide a method by which investors may maximize their return and minimize their risk through the use of **descriptive statistics** as applied to the risk and return of multiple securities. These securities are based on the investor's risk appetite. The theory state that a portfolio may be constructed that **maximizes returns** while **minimizing risk**. It also reinforces the investor's awareness that an acceptance of additional risk will result in higher returns as stated in the Capital Asset Pricing Model. This is achieved through accurate security valuation, asset allocation according to risk appetite (more risk acceptance means more aggressive allocations), portfolio optimization, and the regular measurement of the performance of the portfolio.

Efficient Market Hypothesis

The **Efficient Market Hypothesis** claims that it is impossible for investors to receive returns in excess of normal market returns. The reason for this statement is that stock market efficiency results in share prices that always reflect all current and relevant information. This makes it impossible to purchase undervalued shares or sell shares for inflated amounts. According to the Efficient Market Hypothesis, the only way to achieve greater returns than the market is to take on **additional risk**. Currently, efficient markets are viewed as three types; semi strong, strong, and weak.

Semi strong market efficiency suggests that, while all public information may be included in the valuation of a particular security, not all relevant information about the security is public. Nonpublic information about the stock affects its value and prevents semi strong markets from being truly efficient.

Strong form market efficiency suggests that all information, public and nonpublic, is calculated into the current value of the security. Even inside information would not result in greater-than-normal returns in strongly efficient markets.

Weak form market efficiency asserts that today's price of a security contains information of all of the past prices of the stock. While this theory negates technical analysis, it leaves room for fundamental analysts to find undervalued securities and profit from them.

Portfolio Management Strategies, Styles and Techniques

Strategic Asset Allocation

Strategic asset allocation describes a long-term investing strategy. When risk tolerance and investment goals are determined and suited to the proper portfolio, these securities are held until they are deemed to be no longer suitable or toxic. An allocation of the assets is determined based on the **investor's goal**, and to maintain that allocation, the investor will sell the gains in the highly performing securities and buy more of the underperforming securities to maintain the allocation. This process is called **rebalancing**, so called because is maintains the balance of the allocation. The four parts that make up strategic asset allocation are style, asset class, rebalancing, and buy/hold.

Asset Class

Strategic asset allocation is achieved through understanding the client's goals and risk tolerances and building a portfolio for the client to help him or her meet those goals. **Asset class** describes the different types of securities used to achieve those goals. An investor interested in capital appreciation will allocate a large portion of his or her portfolio to the asset class of equities. An investor interested in capital preservation and current income will place a large allocation of his or her portfolio into the fixed-income securities class. Classes of assets include but are not limited to stocks (or equities), bonds (or fixed income), real estate, and cash.

Rebalancing

Based on the method of investing known as strategic allocation, an allocation of the assets is determined based on the investor's goal, and to maintain that allocation, the investor will sell the gains in the highly performing securities and buy more of the underperforming securities to maintain the allocation. This process is called **rebalancing**, so called because it maintains the balance of the allocation. Rebalancing is an important process to maintain the allocation of the portfolio; without regular rebalancing, certain asset classes may grow or shrink to the point that it effectively changes the strategy of the portfolio. An equity portfolio's bond asset class may overtake the equity allocation and change the objective of the portfolio against the investor's wishes.

Buy and Hold

Buy and hold is an investment strategy whereby the investor buys a particular investment with the goal of **holding** the investment for a long period of time regardless of short-term performance. This strategy is one of the major components of strategic allocation. When risk tolerance and investment goals are determined and suited to the proper portfolio, these securities are held until they are deemed to be no longer suitable. An allocation of the assets is determined based on the investor's goal, and to maintain that allocation, the investor will sell the gains in the highly performing securities and buy more of the underperforming securities to maintain the allocation. While there may be short-term redemption of securities that perform well, the entire holding is not being liquidated, thus securing the buy-and-hold nature of strategic asset allocation.

Tactical Asset Allocation

Tactical asset allocation is a more **active** method of portfolio management than strategic asset allocation. Tactical asset allocation lacks the buy-and-hold component inherent to strategic asset management. More transactions occur in tactical asset allocation that in strategic allocation. This allows the portfolio manager take advantage of current market situations in order to realize **short-term gains**. This strategy is impossible with strategic asset allocation due to its buy-and-hold strategy. Tactical and strategic asset allocations differ in multiple ways. Tactical managers seek short-term profits through multiple transactions throughout the year, whereas strategic managers limit their transactions to rebalances of accounts. Tactical asset allocation is also considered a more active form of account management, while strategic allocation is considered passive portfolio manage.

Style

The **style** of a portfolio that participates in strategic asset allocation refers to the **method** in which the investor's goals are reached. The style applied to each portfolio will differ based on the investor's needs and risk appetites. A retiree with a goal of capital preservation and current income will best be served with a conservative style that allocates much of portfolio's capital to stable, fixed-income securities, such as bonds or bond mutual funds. A young saver, seeking capital appreciation with a large appetite for risk because of his or her ability to absorb and recover risks would be best suited to a portfolio that was heavily allocated in equities with few bonds in the portfolio.

Active vs. Passive Portfolio Management Strategy

Active portfolio management, exemplified in tactical asset allocation, is characterized by **multiple transactions** within a year to take advantage of short-term market conditions to secure gains. **Passive portfolio management**, exemplified by strategic asset allocation, values a **buy-and-hold strategy**, which suggests that stocks historically perform well and will continue to grow in the long term regardless of short-term market movements. Passive portfolio management is marked by few if any transactions during a given year. Most of the transactions seen in passive portfolio management occur due to regular rebalancing of the portfolio's allocation. While active portfolio managers may still try to maintain the portfolio's allocation, this is done with multiple transactions throughout the year in pursuit of short-term gains and often at the rejection of underperforming assets for new assets within the same asset class.

Growth Securities vs. Value Securities

Growth securities are those stocks and bonds of companies that are relatively young and up and coming. They have not proven themselves in the marketplace, but they have a large **potential for growth** as their full potential has not yet been seen. Companies that fall into this category are usually companies with a mid- to small-market capitalization. Because these companies are not well established, they are characterized by greater risk than well-established companies and are more suitable to younger investors seeking capital appreciation. **Value securities** are securities of companies that are **established** and have observable market history. Their business models are well known, and their securities are not volatile and subject to large swings. Companies in this category usually fall into the large-market capitalization and larger categories. The stability and large capitalization of these companies make them suitable investments for older investors seeking stability but some amount of growth. Value stocks also often issue annual dividends.

Income-Producing Securities vs. Capital Appreciation

Income-producing securities are usually characterized by **low-risk, stable securities** that produce some amount of income. Securities that fall into this category include but are not limited to bonds, preferred stocks, real estate investment trusts (REITs), and dividend-paying common stock. Usually, the investor who is most interested in income-producing securities is the retired investor seeking current income and capital preservation. The investor's income need is met by the interest or dividends paid on the securities, and the desire for capital preservation is met because of the stability of the security. Investors seeking **capital appreciation** look to **higher-risk and more volatile securities**, such as common stock of companies that are of small-market capitalization. These investors are usually younger investors with long time horizons, which allow them to absorb losses and benefit from long-term gains.

Portfolio Diversification

Portfolio diversification describes the strategy of diversifying the holdings in a portfolio to hedge against the risk of a market downturn or unexpected loss in an individual security. This is accomplished by holding assets of classes that are **negatively correlated** or have **zero correlation**. The most common form of diversification is shown by investors allocating portions of their portfolio to stocks and other portions to bonds and still others to commodities. If stocks are performing poorly, bonds tend to increase performance (negative correlation), while commodities maintain their performance (zero correlation). Diversification also occurs within asset class to prevent the failure of a single stock from destroying the asset allocation of portfolio. Diversification is important in portfolio allocation as it helps maintain asset allocation and prevents large losses from any single security movement.

Sector Rotation

Sector rotation is the practice of moving invested capital to **different sectors** of the market under the assumption that different sectors of the market are profitable at different points in time. This is helpful to investors who wish exposure to multiple sectors but may not have the initial capital to invest in all the sectors that they desire. Sector rotation is also a method of diversification of the investor's portfolio over a specific time period. Some managers attempt to time the market to make short-term gains through sector rotation, with the assumption that certain sectors are more profitable at different times of the year.

Dollar-Cost Averaging

Dollar-cost averaging describes the practice of regularly investing a fixed amount in a given security, usually a mutual fund, without regard to the **performance** of the investment. This tends to lead to lower investment costs for the investor because the cost is averaged over time, with lower and higher costs offsetting each other. It also results in fewer shares being bought when the market is up and more shares purchased when the market is down, leading to a decreased cost basis in the security. This is helpful to smaller investors because it does not require a large initial outlay in a security to invest successfully as the mutual funds in which they are investing waive the minimum investment required to buy into the fund. The most common occurrence of dollar-cost averaging in the United States is in 401(k) and 403(b) plans.

PUT

A **put** is an options contract between two parties in which the seller guarantees the buyer the right to **sell** a security to the seller of the put at a **set price**, regardless of the current price of the security. Put options may be traded as derivative securities, and as demonstrated in the prior sentence, a lowering of the value of the underlying security makes the value of the put higher. Put contracts are often used to reduce the risk of loss of capital. This is achieved when an investor buys a security and then buys a put contract on the same security. While the investor may want the value of the security to rise, if it loses value then the put will increase in value. If the security rises, then the investor's only loss will be the premium he or she paid for the options contract.

CALL

A **call** is an options contract between two parties in which the seller guarantees the buyer the right to **buy** the underlying security of the call at a **set price**, regardless of the current price of the security. A "**covered call**" is a call contract in which the seller owns the underlying security of the call which he or she is selling. This effectively produces risk-free income for the seller, because if the call is exercised the seller will only have to sell the security from his or her inventory of stocks and then usually at a profit over what was paid for the security. Many managers use this technique to provide risk-free income for retirees and other investors needing current income.

LEVERAGE

Managers who use **leverage** in their management techniques are effectively **borrowing** money to amplify the eventual result of their investment. Without question, leverage greatly increases the risk associated with a portfolio. While this strategy may be appropriate for an investor seeking income, a young and sophisticated investor may be ideally suited to leveraged portfolios and securities. While leverage indeed brings a greater degree of risk, the reward is commensurate with the risk involved. When managers decide to leverage a position, a greater return can be had than would be possible if using only the unleveraged capital available to them. By the same token, leverage can amplify losses, making the losses taken on a security greater than those incurred had they used their own capital.

VOLATILITY

Volatility is the degree to which a security's price has fluctuated (or will fluctuate) within a given time period, whether it has increased or decreased. Volatility can be distinguished between **historical volatility** (HV), which measures the changes in a security's price over a prior time period, and **implied volatility** (IV), which is the estimated degree of volatility for a security's price in the future—what various market factors imply about the security's potential behavior.

Options volatility is the application of volatility measures to options transactions. The premiums for options is related directly to the volatility for the underlying security; higher volatility increases the option premium, and vice versa.

Tax Considerations

Tax Implications Associated with Individual Investing

It is the goal of individuals who invest to receive a return on those investments. According to the United States tax code, those receipts are **taxable income**. Different types of investment income are treated differently under the internal revenue code. **Long-term capital gains**, or those gains obtained from capital appreciation when the security was held for greater than one year, receive a lower tax rate than do **short-term capital gains**. This incentivizes investors to save longer and adopt a less-risky buy-and-hold strategy. Short-term capital gains are taxed at the taxpayer's regular rate of income tax. Capital gains are determined by subtracting the cost basis, or initial investment, from the sales price. There are many factors that affect cost basis. Inherited securities' cost bases are stepped up to the price of the security at the date of the benefactor's death. This, among other things, should always be considered in the calculation of costs basis. Current income, such as dividends and interest received, are treated similarly to short-term gains and taxed at the investor's current tax rate.

Calculation of Gain or Loss

Example 1

Your client purchases 100 shares of a stock on May 1, 2015, for $10 per share. On March 1, 2016, he sells 80 of the shares for $25 per share. Three months later, he sells the remaining shares for $30 per share. Calculate the gain or loss, indicating whether it is short- or long-term.

80 shares sold on March 1st are short-term:

$$Short\ Term\ Gain = (Sales\ Price - Cost\ Basis) \times \#\ of\ Shares$$

$$Short\ Term\ Gain = (25 - 10) \times 80\ shares = \$1{,}200$$

20 shares sold on June 1st are long-term

$$Long\ Term\ Gain = (Sales\ Price - Cost\ Basis) \times \#\ of\ Shares$$

$$Long\ Term\ Gain = (30 - 10) \times 20\ shares = \$400$$

Tax Implication of Holding Various Types of Corporate Bonds

When an investor receives payment based on the coupon of a bond, a taxable event occurs. **Interest payments** received from the coupon of a bond are considered income and are taxed at the taxpayer's normal rate. Any **capital gain** from the sale of a bond that has appreciated is also taxable. If the bond has been held by the investor for greater than one year, the capital gain is considered long term and taxed at the lower long-term capital gains rate. If it has been held for less than a year by the current holder, it will be taxed at the higher short-term capital gains rate, usually the investor's current income tax rate. When a bond is issued at a discount and no interest is physically received, the Internal Revenue Service considers the **accretion of value** (yearly increase up to par value) to be payment of interest and taxable within the year the value is accreted. It is taxed as interest would be taxed at the investor's current tax rate.

AMT

The **alternative minimum tax** is a situation to which an investing taxpayer may find him or herself **liable**. The alternative minimum tax is not a preferable situation for investors as it assesses taxes on income that may have previously been tax advantaged. The alternative minimum tax was written into the Internal Revenue code to prevent abuse of tax-advantaged investments by those with the means to do so. Such exemptions of income earned and deductions that are disallowed include but are not limited to accelerated depreciation, tax-exempt interest on certain types of municipal bonds, and tax-advantaged employee stock options. The tax advantages of the previous examples are disallowed, which raises the taxpayer's taxable income and results in a higher tax bill.

Corporate, Trust, and Estate Income Taxation

Corporate taxation is handled separately for the two different types of corporations. **S-Corporations** are not taxed, but the individual or individuals to whom the income from the S-Corporation flowed are taxed. To many, this is preferable to the taxation of the C-Corporation. **C-Corporations** are taxed at the corporate level and then again when the profits are distributed to the shareholders. Many corporations prefer to have the S-Corporation structure, but laws allow only for only 100 or fewer shareholders of S-Corporations. Trusts are legal entities set up to ensure the execution of the trustor's, or the person contributing assets, wishes. **Trusts** must pay taxes annually similarly to individuals. In many cases, individuals with trusts pay a very low amount of tax as their trust holds most of their assets and receives income from those assets. The trust must then pay the taxes that the individual would have normally incurred. **Estates** are not taxable until the death of the person holding the estate. At that point, proceeds from the estate, in the form of inheritances given, are taxed.

The **estate tax** is a tax levied on the transfer of significant assets when the original owner of the assets dies. Entire estates may be transferred without incurring estate tax to spouses who are citizens of the United States. The estate tax is calculated based upon the amount of the estate after the transfer of the estate to the spouse, contributions to charitable organizations, and satisfaction of the deceased's debts. This number is called the **adjusted gross estate**, or **AGE**. The AGE number is used to calculate the tax on the amounts passed on to heirs and other recipients of the deceased's estate. Investors can reduce AGE by contributing large amounts to charitable organizations and by passing their entire estates to their spouses.

Gift Tax

The **gift tax** is a federal tax applied to anything of value that a person may give to another person. This usually applies to large cash gifts, and there are several **exclusions**. Items that are usually excluded from the gift tax include gifts to spouses, gifts to political organizations, gifts that fall under the annual gift tax exclusion amount, and payment of medical or educational expenses. Investors may plan for the gift tax by considering to whom the gift is being given. Gifts to family members are treated differently than normal gifts. The use of trusts to gift assets or money is also useful in the legal avoidance of gift tax. In this manner, the person giving the gift is not the legal giver per the Internal Revenue Code.

Retirement Plans

Taxation of Retirement Plans

Retirement plans are taxed-advantaged accounts whereby investors may save earnings to plan for their eventual retirement. The tax benefits of retirement plans were legislatively approved to incentivize younger workers to save for retirement, as Social Security was thought to not adequately meet the needs of future retirees and fewer companies were offering defined benefit plans, such as pensions. Retirement savings plans vary widely as to contribution limits and taxation. Most retirement plans allow investors to **defer** the taxation of their incomes and earnings on the investments of the retirement plans until they're withdrawn after age 59 ½. This benefits the investor by reducing their current income and tax liability. Other retirement accounts, called **Roth**

accounts, are funded by after-tax dollars, and the investments grow tax free and are not taxed at withdrawal.

Traditional Individual Retirement Accounts

The most common of the retirement accounts is the **individual retirement account**, or the **IRA**. IRAs are usually funded by investors with after-tax dollars, and then a tax deduction is granted to the investor in the same year that the investor made the contribution. This effectively makes the money invested pretax dollars. The investments, dividends, and interest are allowed to grow tax free until the investor begins to take distributions. At that point, all distributions are taxed as current income. To encourage retirement saving, a 10 percent penalty payable to the Internal Revenue Service is assessed on distributions taken before age 59 ½. A **required minimum distribution**, or **RMD**, must be taken by IRA holders after age 72, or a penalty of one half of the RMD will be assessed to the IRA holder. As of 2023, contributions are limited to $6,500 a year or $7,500 a year to investors age 50 and over. Contributions to IRAs must come from earned income.

Roth-Contribution Individual Retirement Accounts

Roth-contribution Individual Retirement Accounts (IRAs) are much like traditional IRAs in their contribution components. As of 2023, a maximum of $6,500 annually may be contributed by investors under the age of 50, and $7,500 annually may be contributed by investors over 50. Roth accounts, unlike traditional IRAs, are funded with **after-tax dollars**. While the investor receives no tax benefit at the time of contribution, as is the case with traditional IRAs, the investments' capital appreciation, interest, and dividends grow tax free, and no taxes are applied to the distributions that the investor takes. Similar to traditional IRAs, Roth IRA holders may not take distributions before 59 ½ without submitting to a penalty, but unlike traditional IRAs, there is no required minimum distribution starting at age 70 ½ because the funds have already been taxed. Roth IRAs must be funded with earned income.

Qualified Retirement Plans

Qualified retirement plans are **tax-advantaged savings plans** that are given legislative reprieve from certain taxes. These advantages were placed on the plans to encourage workers to save for retirement. Examples of such benefits include reduction of taxable income, tax-deferred earnings and growth, and in some cases, tax-free earnings and growth. Because of the tax-advantaged nature of the retirement plans, there are limits placed upon the amount of income that may be tax deferred. Each plan's contribution limit varies. To prevent abuse of tax-advantaged retirement plans by wealthy individuals, the legislation that allows for the use of retirement plans requires that the contributions to the plans be earned income and not capital gains or interest received. Qualified retirement plans are typically call-defined contribution plans.

Pension and Profit Sharing

Pensions are a type of qualified retirement plan in which the recipient's employer contributes assets to the plan on behalf of the employee. These funds are then invested for the employee to provide the employee with retirement income. As the employee does not contribute to pensions plans, pensions are typically referred to as **defined benefit plans**, referring to their nature as a benefit of employment. **Profit-sharing plans** are benefit plans whereby the employer shares the profits of the business with the employees. Profit-sharing can be contributed to qualified plans and deferred for the benefit of the employees' retirement incomes or paid directly to the employees.

401(k) Plans

401(k) plans, so named in reference to the section of the Internal Revenue Code that governs such accounts, are **employer-sponsored, tax-advantaged** retirement plans. 401(k) plans were legislatively given tax preference to encourage small investors to save for retirement. Many investors without sophistication or access to investment planning benefit from 401(k) plans because they are made available to all employees that meet certain eligibility requirements of a company that has implemented a 401(k) plan. 401(k) plans are funded with pretax dollars, and taxation is deferred until the investor begins taking distributions. At that point, all distributions are taxed as current income. To encourage retirement saving, a 10 percent penalty payable to the Internal Revenue Service is assessed on distributions taken before age 59 ½. A required minimum distribution, or RMD, must be taken by 401(k) holders after age 70 ½, or a penalty of one half of the RMD will be assessed to the 401(k) holder. As of 2023, the maximum contribution to a 401(k) plan is $22,500 or $30,000 if the investor is age 50 or older.

403(b) Plans

403 (b) plans, so named in reference to the section of the Internal Revenue Code that governs such accounts, are employer-sponsored, tax-advantaged retirement plans. These employers must be **nonprofit organizations**. 403(b) plans are often equated with 401(k) plans. 403(b) plans were legislatively given tax preference to encourage small investors to save for retirement. Many investors without sophistication or access to investment planning benefit from 403(b) plans because they are made available to all employees that meet certain eligibility requirements of a company that has implemented a 403(b) plan. 403(b) plans are funded with pretax dollars, and taxation is deferred until the investor begins taking distributions. At that point, all distributions are taxed as current income. To encourage retirement saving, a 10 percent penalty payable to the Internal Revenue Service is assessed on distributions taken before age 59 ½. A required minimum distribution, or RMD, must be taken by IRA holders after age 70 ½, or a penalty of one half of the RMD will be assessed to the IRA holder. As of 2023, the maximum contribution to a 403(b) plan is $22,500 or $30,000 if the investor is age 50 or older.

Nonqualified Retirement Plans

Nonqualified retirement plans are those plans that are not governed by the Employee Retirement Income Security Act, or **ERISA**. As such, they are not required to follow the guidelines and laws established therein. While this exemption from ERISA allows the plan sponsors and plan holders to structure the plans to benefit key individuals and avoid granting the same benefits to all employees; the exemption from ERISA also prevents the investors in the plan from receiving tax deductions based upon any contributions to the plan. Additionally, the contributions to the plans on the employee's behalf are often treated as taxable income. Although the plans do not allow a tax deduction to be taken, they are allowed to grow tax deferred. Nonqualified retirement plans are often seen in the execution of deferred compensation plans and bonuses to executives.

ERISA Issues

ERISA

The **Employee Retirement Income Security Ac**t, or **ERISA**, regulates the creation and administration of retirement plans and corporate pensions and sets standards that must be maintained for both types of plans. ERISA was enacted to protect the rights of individual investors. Per ERISA, all profit-sharing plans and corporate pensions must be established through the use of a trust. Trustees are then appointed and assume fiduciary duty in the administration of the plan. ERISA provides tax incentives for employees to save money for retirement. These incentives come in the form of income reduction (thus tax reduction) and deferral of taxation on investment earnings in the ERISA plans.

FIDUCIARY

The term **fiduciary** dictates that those in a position of responsibility for the funds and assets of others always act in the **best interest** of those whom they represent. A fiduciary has legal responsibility of a given client's funds and is under a moral imperative to act in the client's best interests. Section 404(c) of the Employee Retirement Income Security Act (ERISA) gives explicit requirements for those in fiduciary roles pertaining to retirement plans. Among these requirements are for the fiduciary party to act fully in accordance with the plan document. Fiduciaries may delegate duties in the administration of the plan, but under no circumstances may the fiduciary duties be delegated. According to section 404 (c) of ERISA, fiduciaries must always act in the best interests of the plan and to provide benefits to the plan and its participants. They must be diligent in the management of the plan and show that they administer the plan with a high level of expertise. Among these duties is for the fiduciary to ensure that the plan is properly diversified to reduce the risk of large losses.

INVESTMENT POLICY STATEMENTS

Investment policy statements are written guidelines that instruct the fiduciary of the given plan on the **funding** of the plan and how the fiduciary should **manage** the investment decisions. In short, investment policy statements are written statements that specify the needs of a plan. The policy statement should include the plan's investment objectives, determine how cash flow needs should be met, set forth the plan's investment philosophy, especially regarding asset allocation and management style, the criteria upon which the selection of investments will be based, and outline a system for monitoring the performance of the plan and adherence to processes set forth in the plan.

PROHIBITED TRANSACTIONS

Dealing in **prohibited transactions** creates a clear **conflict of interest** for the fiduciary party of an Employee Retirement Income Security Act retirement plan. The definition of fiduciary negates the allowance of any conflicts of interest. Transactions that fiduciaries are prohibited from executing include but are not limited to self-dealing, or managing the plans funds to benefit the fiduciary's own accounts; involving the plan assets in a transaction while acting on the behalf of a person, natural, or legal whose goals work counter to the goals of the plan as outlined in the plan's policy statement; and accepting remuneration for the private account of the fiduciary that results from transactions involving the plan for which they are the fiduciary party.

Special Types of Accounts

529 ACCOUNTS

Section 529 plans, also known as **qualified tuition plans**, are college savings investment plans that are administered by each state. There are two types of 529 plans. The prepaid tuition plan allows investors to pay college tuition, and occasionally room and board, in advance and effectively lock in the current tuition rates so that the beneficiary may attend regardless of tuition rates at the time that they attend college. The college savings plan allows contributors to name a beneficiary and contribute to the plan on his or her behalf; the contribution limits vary by state but tend to be high. The contributions are allowed to grow tax free, and all distributions are tax free as long as they are for qualified educational expenses. Any nonqualified distribution will be subject to taxation on earnings and a 10 percent penalty. Any unused portion of the 529 plan may be passed to a member of the beneficiary's immediate family without incurring penalties and taxes on earnings. Additionally, with the SECURE Act of 2019, 529 plan funds can pay up to $10,000 in student loan debt.

Coverdell Education Accounts

Coverdell education savings accounts are tax-advantaged savings plans that allow investors to plan for expenses associated with **education**. While the contributions must be made with after-tax dollars, the earnings received on a Coverdell account are not taxable as long as they are used for qualified education expenses. Any withdrawal of funds not related to educational purposes will result in the taxation of any gains and a 10 percent penalty assessed to the investor based upon the amount withdrawn. As of 2023, the maximum annual contribution to a Coverdell education savings account is $2,000. Also, as of 2023, certain brackets of wage earners are not allowed to participate in Coverdell savings accounts. Married persons filing jointly may not earn more than $190,000 in a single year before the phaseout of benefits begins. Single taxpayers may not earn more than $95,000 before the phaseouts begin.

Uniform Gift to Minors Act Accounts and Uniform Transfer to Minors Act Accounts

The **Uniform Gift to Minors Act** created a way in which property could be legally given to minors. These types of accounts were later replaced by the **Uniform Transfer to Minors Act**. The regulations governing Uniform Transfer to Minors tend to be more flexible than those governing Uniform Gift to Minors. When the law was modified to the *Transfer* language, properties other than gifts were allowed to be transferred to the account of the minor. These two types of accounts are **custodial accounts**, thus requiring a custodian to buy and sell securities in the account, exercise rights and warrants in the account, and make decisions to buy, sell, or hold the securities placed in the minor's account. The custodian on the account is required until the child reaches the age of majority.

HSAs

Health savings accounts (HSAs) are accounts designed for people with **high-deductible health plans** (HDHPs). These accounts allow tax-deductible contributions which are then used to pay for qualified medical expenses not covered by the health plans. Moreover, any investment in the account grows tax-free, and there are no taxes on distributions, so long as they are used for qualified medical expenses.

Ownership and Estate Planning Techniques

JTWROS

Joint tenants with rights of survivorship, or **JTWROS**, are jointly owned accounts in which the interest of one of the owners is thought to be identical to the interests of the other owner. If one of the parties dies, the surviving party retains his or her portion of the account and receives the entire portion of the account that the deceased owned. Accounts registered as JTWROS are most commonly utilized by husbands and wives as there interests usually are identical, and the beneficial arrangement of payment on death does not usually create a conflict with other parties.

TIC Accounts

Accounts registered as **tenants-in-common**, or **TIC accounts**, are a type of joint account. TIC accounts are made up of two or individuals that agree to share an investment account but do not wish for the other party to receive their assets in the case of their demise. Upon the passing of one of the account owners, that owner's share of the assets is passed to the owner's estate, and all outstanding transactions and orders are immediately cancelled. Tenants-in-common is a common designation for joint accounts held by business partners, siblings, friends, and most investing partners who are not spouses. This is done because usually non-spouse investing partners do not have significantly identical interests and goals, as do spouses.

Tenants by the Entirety

Tenancy by the entirety is a form of shared property ownership for married couples only. It allows for spouses to own property as a single entity. Each spouse has an equal, undivided interest and has a right of survivorship. If one spouse dies, the other automatically has full ownership of the property. The condition of mutual ownership means that both spouses need to be in agreement when making decisions about use of the property (i.e., one can't sell all or part of the property without consent of the other).

POD Accounts

The designation of an account registered as **payable-on-death**, or alternatively as **transfer-on-death**, provides an easy method to keep an investor's funds and securities from being subjected to the probate courts upon the death of the current owner. The account owner names a beneficiary to receive the assets held in his or her brokerage account upon the death of the account owner and registers the account as transfer-on-death to the beneficiary. It is widely regarded as the easiest way to ensure that a beneficiary receives assets without going through the probate process, and the process is also usually completed without any additional costs. Transfer-on-death should not be the sole method by which inheritances are coordinated, but they are very efficient and helpful in estate planning.

Trust and Estate Accounts

Trust and estate accounts are managed almost identically. The main difference in the accounts is that estate accounts are set up to manage a deceased person's estate. **Trust accounts** are those accounts that are owned by a trust that is acting as a legal entity. Trusts are used by investors to simplify the transference of property to beneficiaries after the investor's death. **Estates** that are governed by trusts usually avoid probate court altogether and allow more assets to be passed on by avoiding fees associated with probate court. Trust accounts further simplify the process by allowing the trust to possess ownership of the investment account and name the beneficiary at account registration. Thus, trust accounts provide multiple benefits to investors by bypassing probate (and saving fees associated therewith) and providing an easy method of transference to the beneficiary.

Qualified Domestic Relations Orders

Qualified domestic relations orders (QDROs) concern the division of property following a divorce, specifically the division of a retirement plan. A QDRO is a court order based on a **divorce settlement** which allots a portion of the retirement or pension plan to family members, ordinarily to the accountholder's ex-spouse but sometimes also to children or dependents. The most ordinary QDRO allotment is 50% of the total increase in the retirement plan's assets from the marriage's inception to the point of divorce. QDROs are important because they also shift tax liability. If an accountholder were simply to distribute a portion of his retirement account to his ex-spouse, the accountholder would still be liable for the taxes, but a QDRO ensures that the ex-spouse would be liable.

Trading Securities

Bids, Offers, and Quotes

A quote is given by market makers as a bid and an offer on a specific security. These are often referred to as **firm quotes**. Dealers set the highest price at which they will buy a security; this is referred to as the **current bid**. Dealers also set the lowest price at which they will sell that same security, referred to as the **current offer**. The difference between the two is called the **spread**, or markup. The spread exists so that the dealer may make money for services provided. This affects the final trading price by effectively imposing a small premium on each transaction.

Market Order, Limit Order, and Stop Order

There are many tools at an investor's disposal when trading securities. If an investor desires to trade immediately at the current level of the market, he or she will place a **market order** and accept the next price for which they can buy or sell the desired security. No restrictions are placed on market orders. **Limit orders** help investors time their transactions according to market movements without having to constantly watch the security for the right price. A limit order will execute a buy or sell if the price reaches the desired level but will not execute if the price fluctuates past the desired levels. **Stop orders**, similar to limit orders, help the investor with timing. The stop level is essentially a trigger point in the securities price. Unlike a limit, however, once desired level is reached, the very next price will be accepted regardless of the next price.

Short Sale

Short sales are speculative investments whereby an investor attempts to profit from the **decline** in value of a given security. To accomplish this, the investor borrows securities from a broker's inventory and sells that security on the market. The investor must then replace the security in the broker's inventory. If the price of the security decreases, the investor has made a return commensurate with the decline in price of the security sold short. If the price rises, the investor will lose money commensurate with the gain of the security, which is theoretically limitless. Short sales are risky speculative investments and should only be attempted by sophisticated investors.

Cash Accounts and Margin Accounts

Cash accounts are the most common types of brokerage accounts. They are used by most investors for their simplicity and low risk as an account type. Cash accounts are acceptable accounts for all investor types. Gains in cash accounts are limited by the amount of capital available to the investor. **Margin accounts** are accounts whereby investors have access to loanable funds, or leverage. The loanable funds are used to magnify gains but have the potential to magnify losses. Investors have the potential to increase the gain in margin accounts by borrowing extra capital to invest and paying it back from the extra gains earned from the extra capital invested. This process works in reverse with losses in margin accounts, increasing the potential for losses. The investor must also pay a rate of interest on the loaned funds in a margin account. Only sophisticated and experienced investors who understand the implications of margin accounts and seek speculative gains should use margin accounts.

Trade as a Principal and Trade as an Agent

A trader selling securities from his or her own inventory and acting on his or her own behalf is acting as a dealer in the role of a **principal**. A principal or dealer's profit motive is satisfied by the capital gains and trading fees he or she may acquire due to the transactions between the principal and the principal's clients. A trader acting on behalf of a client or dealer is known as a broker, acting in the role of an **agent**. The broker may be an agent either for a dealer or for a client. A broker's profit motive is satisfied by the commission he or she earns as a result of the sale and through fees charged. Principals act on their own behalf; agents act on the behalf of others.

High-Frequency Trading

High-frequency trading (HFT) is a type of automatic trading which uses technology, computers in particular, to process high quantities of orders and transactions at extremely fast speeds. Such trading utilizes algorithms to compile and apply data from several different markets and to assess market conditions. Although HFT systems have been acknowledged to improve market liquidity, such systems have received criticism for removing the human element of practical judgment from stock trading and for crowding out smaller traders given the economic advantages such trading confers on the larger companies who can afford to implement HFT.

Dark Pools of Liquidity

For some orders, the volume of securities traded can be hidden from public knowledge. This is usually done by institutional investors, to keep their trades secret from other (competing) institutional investors. These types of trades are said to involve **dark pools of liquidity**, since the actual trades are concealed or cloudy.

Broker-Dealer

Broker-dealers are people or companies that trade securities on their **own behalf** (dealer) and also operate as **go-betweens** for other clients (brokers). Broker-dealers must be registered with the Securities Exchange Commission. Because brokers only complete transactions for other persons and dealers only transact business for themselves, firms that perform both actions are called broker-dealers. Broker-dealers facilitate trading for clients that otherwise would not have been able to have access to the market while, at the same time, trading for their own accounts. While the capacity in which the broker-dealer acts depends upon the transaction, occasionally broker-dealers act as both brokers and dealers when they sell securities held to their current clientele.

Specialists

Specialists are persons (natural or legal) that act as **market makers** to enable trading of a given security. Specialists possess inventories of that stock to sell in the absence of a selling investor or orders that are too large to fill based on the amount currently for sell by individual investors. Specialists also facilitate trading by posting the bid and ask prices of the stock for which they make the market. They also execute orders placed with limits and trades in general. Generally, it is the role of specialists to wait in reserve to fill or receive orders of their given securities to guarantee a stable and fair market.

Market Makers

Market makers are brokers or broker-dealers who retain large holdings of specific securities and are on standby to buy or sell those securities according to the current bid/ask prices. Market makers play a vital role in providing **liquidity** for the financial markets by buying or selling the specific securities for which they are responsible when there is no general supply or demand, thus "making the market." They also promote general efficiency on stock exchanges by promoting ease of trading via their market making tendencies. While brokers typically handle market making responsibilities, the two business transactions are separate forms of business and must remain as such to prevent conflicts of interest instigated by a broker recommending securities based on the market the firm makes.

Security Exchanges

Securities exchanges are organizations by which stocks, bonds, options, commodities, futures, and other securities are bought and sold. Securities exchanges provide the **infrastructure** needed for investors to trade securities efficiently and prevent administrative errors from stopping the flow of assets and money. Strict compliance with Securities Exchange Commission regulations are addressed by the major United States securities exchanges, and transparency is maintained thereby. Without efficient securities exchanges, investors would be unable to make reliable and stable trades, making investing in the markets less attractive and resulting in less capital investment for economic expansion. The major securities exchanges in the United States are the New York Stock Exchange (NYSE), the Chicago Board of Options Exchange (CBOE), the NASDAQ, and the NYSE MKT LLC (formerly the NYSE Amex).

Auction Markets

Auction markets are arrangements where prospective buyers and prospective sellers compete with another to make **bids** and **offers**. Securities traded in auction markets will naturally be traded according to the highest bid and lowest ask price. The execution of orders in auction markets involves matching compatible bids and asks.

Examples of auction markets include the Philadelphia Stock Exchange (NASDAQ OMX PHLX), NYSE Euronext, NYSE MKT LLC (formerly NYSE Amex Equities), and NYSE Arca.

Stock Market

Stock markets are the mediums by which the trade of equity securities is facilitated and are sometimes called **equity markets**. All trading of public stocks occurs on stock markets. Stock markets provide investors with access to shares in the ownership of publicly traded companies and provide those publicly traded companies a means by which they may have access to the capital that investors wish to make available. Initial issues of stocks, also called initial public offerings, or capitals, are traded on the **primary market**. These issues are purchased by institutional investors for sale to retail investors on the **secondary market**. Most small investors do not have access to the primary market and are aided in their purchases by the existence of a secondary market.

OTC Markets

Stocks that trade in some manner other than via a traditional stock exchange are said to be traded "**over the counter**." These securities are usually traded over a dealer network rather than a centralized exchange such as the New York Stock Exchange. Because there is not necessarily a large market for OTC stocks, and no specialists or market makers as with large stock exchanges, OTC stocks can be very **illiquid**, and investors in such stocks should consider the liquidity risks of stocks purchased over the counter. The best-known example of an OTC market is the NASDAQ. It is an electronic trading exchange that is not considered to be a formal exchange. Many companies listed on major exchanges pay to be listed on the NASDAQ for ease of trading. These companies' stocks are not considered traditional OTC stock, but are traded OTC.

The **over-the-counter (OTC) market** is also known as the **second market** (not to be confused with the secondary market, which encompasses all the various ways of trading stock besides new issues). It consists of a nationwide network of brokers and dealers connected by phone and computer who trade non-listed stocks from their offices. NASDAQ, Bulletin Board, and Pink Sheet stocks comprise the second market, with the most prominent distinction being between NASDAQ issues and non-NASDAQ issues.

Commissions Allowed on Securities Transactions

Commissions are monies paid to a broker or agent to facilitate a trade on the behalf of another investor, usually a small retail investor. Commissions present the advisor with an ethical minefield to navigate. One example of unethical practices concerning commissions is a practice known as churning. **Churning** is the practice of making multiple and unnecessary trades in a client's account for the sole purpose of generating commissions. Collecting reasonable commissions is a perfectly legal and ethical manner of transacting business. Unreasonable commissions, however, are not. **Unreasonable commissions** usually describe a situation whereby an unreasonable amount of profit is made but may also occur when a broker sells a security much higher than the actual value of the security, even if he or she is not making a large profit because of it. This may happen because the broker paid a higher price for the security and the security has been underperforming.

Markups

The term **markup** as it pertains to securities trading describes the amount of money over the original purchase price that a broker charges the purchasing party. The markup is very important to the seller because it is the only means by which a **profit** is made on those business transactions. Investors pay the markup as a fee for facilitating their trading needs. **Unreasonable markups** are unethically high markups. Markups are determined to be unreasonable if they are unusually higher than most other markups on other transactions that are significantly similar. Very high markups that are due to capital gains are not considered unreasonable as long as the security is still traded closely to the market value.

Spread

The **spread**, as it applies to securities trading, refers to the difference obtained by subtracting the **bid**, or the highest amount that the broker will pay for a security, from the **ask**, or the lowest amount that the broker will accept for the security. The spread is usually an effective means by which the markup can be calculated; however, if the broker has held the security that is offered for sale for an extended length of time, it may not be a good measurement of the markup. The spread can be affected by many different dynamics. If a security is in high demand or is of low supply, the spread may be large to fairly compensate the broker for the effort required in obtaining the security for sale.

Best Execution

Best Execution refers to the legal requirement put upon brokers to provide customers the most advantageous order execution given the current market environment. Brokers have choices about trades and how they are executed, including the use of services that offer incentives for routing trades through them. Best execution ensures that brokers are putting the best interest of their clients' ahead of their own when it comes to trade execution. Both the Security and Exchange Commission (SEC) and Financial Industry Regulatory Authority (FINRA) regularly examine brokers best execution practices.

Portfolio Performance Measures

Risk-Adjusted Return and the Modern Portfolio Theory

Risk-adjusted return is a measurement of the rate of return of a security or a portfolio of securities based on the **risk** inherent in the investments made. Theoretically, and according to modern portfolio theory, if investors accept higher risk, their return should be commensurate. The return of a portfolio with high returns and a high degree of risk may be observed more accurately when it is risk adjusted. The same can be said of low-risk portfolios with low returns. The risk-adjusted concept applies concepts of **modern portfolio theory** when determining risk-adjusted returns. These concepts include Alpha (return), Beta (risk), R-Squared (correlation), Standard Deviation (volatility), and the Sharpe ratio (excessive risk). These measurements are applied to the return of the investment to obtain a more valid metric of return.

Risk-Adjusted Return

Risk-adjusted return describes a measurement of the return of a portfolio or security that has been adjusted based upon the risk inherent to that portfolio or security. The risk-adjusted return is usually measured by the **Sharpe ratio**. The Sharpe ratio of a given portfolio or security is found by subtracting the risk-free rate, or the rate of return based on an investment in which there is little expectation of risk (usually Treasuries), and dividing that number by the standard deviation of the portfolio. The Sharpe ratio is indicative of the quantity of return compared to the amount of risk taken. It is important for an investor to understand the risk-adjusted return to understand that higher-than-normal returns may in fact be due to higher-than-normal risk, which could damage the returns of the portfolio or security at a later time.

Example 1

Calculate the Sharpe ratio for an investment with the following properties:

Portfolio Return = 7.5%
Risk Free Rate of Return = 2.5%
Standard Deviation of Portfolio Return = .06

Sharpe Ratio = 0.83

Example 2

A portfolio has a Sharpe ratio of 1.5. The portfolio returned 10% and the risk-free rate is 2.5%. Based on this information, what is the standard deviation of portfolio return?

Standard deviation of portfolio return = 0.05

Time-Weighted Return

Time-weighted return is a technique of assessing the returns of a portfolio without considering client withdrawals or contributions from or to the account. Reinvestments of capital gains and dividends and interest paid are also excluded from the time-weighted rate of return calculation. This provides the investor with an **internal rate of return** to compare to the current rate of return and assess if the account actually performing better or worse than the current rate of return. The time-weighted rate of return is sometimes also referred to as the **geometric mean return**, because it is taken by calculating the geometric mean among the various time periods under consideration, although without counting any inflows or outflows of cash in the investment as part of the return.

Example 1

A portfolio is valued at $5,000 at the start of year 1. At the end of year 1, a further cash investment of $1,000 is made, making the portfolio's investment at that point to be $6,600. At the end of year 2, a $1,500 cash investment is made, making the portfolio at that point to be $8,500. At the end of year 3, a $1,200 cash investment is made, making the portfolio at that point to be $10,000. Calculate the time-weighted return on this investment.

Return for year 1 = ($6,600 - $1,000) / $5,000 – 1 = 12.00%
Return for year 2 = ($8,500 - $1,500) / $6,600 – 1 = 6.06%
Return for year 3 = ($10,000 - $1,200) / $8,500 – 1 = 3.53%

Geometric mean for these returns (1+R):

$$(1.12 \times 1.0606 \times 1.0353)^{\frac{1}{3}} = 1.0714$$

Time-weighted return = 1.0714 – 1 = 7.14%

Example 2

A mutual fund investment is valued at $200 at the start of the year. At the end of March, a further cash investment of $1,000 is made, making the investment at that point to be $1,275. At the end of June, a $500 cash investment is made, making the portfolio at that point to be $1,675. At the end of September, a $300 cash investment is made, making the portfolio at that point to be $2,000. At the end of the year, the portfolio is worth $2,350. Calculate the time-weighted return on this investment.

Return for first quarter = ($1,275 - $1,000) / $200 – 1 = 37.50%
Return for second quarter = ($1,675 - $500) / $1,275 – 1 = -7.84%
Return for third quarter = ($2,000 - $300) / $1,675 – 1 = 1.49%
Return for fourth quarter = $2,350 / $2,000 – 1 = 17.5%

Geometric mean for these returns (1+R):

$$(1.375 \times 0.9216 \times 1.0149 \times 1.175)^{\frac{1}{4}} = 1.1087$$

Time-weighted return = 1.1087 – 1 = 10.87%

Dollar-Weighted Return

Dollar-weighted return, or **internal rate of return (IRR)**, is used for comparison purposes against the current rate of return. Dollar-weighted returns are adjusted for cash flows into and out of a portfolio based on a net present value of zero. This helps the investor determine if the investment is worth making based on the future cash flows of this investment versus the cash flows available with other investments. The dollar-weighted return evaluation is important in helping creating a metric by which cash flows may be assessed to determine the viability of an investment opportunity.

Example

On January 1, 2015, your client invests $100,000 in Investment A. On July 1, 2015, he invests an additional $50,000 in the investment, and he also gains a dividend of $1,000 but does not reinvest it. On the one-year anniversary of the initial purchase, the value of the account is $160,000. Your client wants to know how much money his account earned over the previous year. Calculate the dollar-weighted return (i.e., internal rate of return [IRR]).

IRR is the rate at which the present value of all future cash inflows equals the investment's cash outflows. In this example, the $100,000 and $50,000 contributions are both cash outflows for the investor, while the final account valuation can be deemed as an outflow. For this formula, notice that the time period is broken down into six-month periods, such that the year-end value is the value after 2 periods.

$$0 = -100{,}000 - \frac{50{,}000}{1+R} + \frac{1{,}000}{1+R} + \frac{160{,}000}{(1+R)^2}$$

$$100{,}000(1+R)^2 + 50{,}000(1+R) - 1{,}000(1+R) - 160{,}000 = 0$$

$$100{,}000(R^2 + 2R + 1) + 49{,}000 + 49{,}000R - 160{,}000 = 0$$

$$100{,}000R^2 + 249{,}000R - 11{,}000 = 0$$

R = 4.34%, but each period was semiannual, so R must be annualized

$$IRR = (1 + R)^2 - 1 \approx 8.87\%$$

Annualized Return

Annualized returns are a measurement of the expected return if an investor would have held an investment for an entire **year**. Annualized returns are calculated by multiplying the return of a security or portfolio by an annualization factor, or one year divided by the total number of days the security or portfolio was held. Annualized returns are useful measurements in that they can provide a rough assumption of expected annual returns of a security without having to hold the security for an entire year. However, investment decisions should not be based solely on annualization of securities as past performance is never indicative of future returns.

Total Return

The **total return** of an investment includes dividends, interest, and capital gain, in addition to capital appreciation, evaluated annually. In this way, losses may be offset by dividends or interest. The current rate of return may not be accurate because of the discounting of these factors. This method is often considered to be the **most accurate measure** of how a certain asset may have performed for an investor. Investors assessing the value and performance of holdings should always take into account the total return of a security. What may appear to be an underperforming security at first glance may be actually be a very good investment. Bonds are a classic example of securities whose performance is not actually shown in capital appreciation, and total return should be considered to provide a more complete picture of performance. The real value of the bond may be in the income it provides.

Example 1

Calculate the total return for a stock investment that was purchased for $500, sold for $650, and returned $80 in dividend income while the investor held the stock.

Expressed an absolute dollar amount, the total return would be the numerator of the above fraction, or $230.

Example 2

Calculate the total return for a bond with a face value of $1,000, a 2% coupon rate (paid annually), and a life of 5 years, if that bond is held to maturity.

Expressed an absolute dollar amount, the total return would be the numerator of the above fraction, or $100.

Holding Period Return

Holding period return describes the return that an asset or portfolio experiences during the length of time the investor held the investments. All dividends, interest, and capital gains received during that period of time are included in the return calculation. This provides the investor with an accurate view of the **performance** of the security. Holding period return is essentially a calculation of total return but as related to a specific holding period, whereas total return is measured annually. Given this fact, holding period return is not annualized. Nonannualized returns are often difficult to compare to other returns. This should be remembered when using the holding period return method of performance evaluation.

Internal Rate of Return

Internal rates of return are discount rates by which investors determine the **viability** of taking on new investments. Internal rates of return take many factors into consideration, especially the time value of money. If the internal rate of return is calculated to be positive and higher than the rate that the investor requires from an investment, the investor accepts the investment. The internal rate of return calculation is most applicable to the bond market as there are regular cash flows to measure and compare with a set maturity. Investors find these measurements helpful in determining the proper course when presented with two seemingly identical investments.

Example 1

An individual purchases an investment for $2,000. The investment will pay out $500 at the end of the first year, $1,000 at the end of the second year, and one final payment of $1,500 at the end of the third year. Based on this payment schedule, is the IRR greater than or less than 20%?

$$\text{Year 1: } PV = \frac{\$500}{1.20^1} = \$416.67$$

$$\text{Year 2: } PV = \frac{1{,}000}{1.20^2} = \$694.44$$

$$\text{Year 3: } PV = \frac{1{,}500}{1.20^3} = \$868.06$$

$$-2{,}000 + 416.67 + 694.44 + 868.06 = -\$20.83$$

The IRR is the discount rate at which all the investment's outflows and inflows add up to $0, so the IRR for this investment is below 20%.

Example 2

An individual purchased an investment. The investment will pay out $10,000 at the end of the first year, $10,000 at the end of the second year, and one final payment of $5,500 at the end of the third year. The IRR is 11%. How much was the initial investment?

$$\text{Year 1: } PV = \frac{10{,}000}{1.11^1} = \$9{,}009$$

$$\text{Year 2: } PV = \frac{10{,}000}{1.11^2} = \$8{,}116$$

$$\text{Year 3: } PV = \frac{5{,}500}{1.11^3} = \$4{,}022$$

$$-x + 9{,}009 + 8{,}116 + 4{,}022 = 0$$

$$x = \$21{,}147 \ \textit{initial investment}$$

Expected Return

Expected rates of return are not based upon empirical data, as are historical returns or actual rates of return. Expected returns are the **estimates of return** that an investor expects to receive from an asset based on the probability of that asset returning several different rates. Expected rates of return help the investor identify which securities are worth the capital outlay based on the expected rate of return versus differing levels of risk. The most basic function of expected return is to assess if an investment will produce positive or negative results. Expected rates of return should not be the sole consideration when determining suitable investments.

EXAMPLE 1

Calculate the expected return for an investor who expects his portfolio to have the following annual returns:

Bonds (10% of portfolio): 2%
Large Cap Stocks (30% of portfolio): 5%
Small Cap Stocks (40% of portfolio): 10%
Foreign Stocks (20% of portfolio): 8%

Expected Return = 7.3%

EXAMPLE 2

An investor holds two stocks, $400 in Stock A and $800 in Stock B. The expected return for Stock A is 5% and the expected return for the combined stocks is 7.5%. Calculate the expected return for Stock B.

Total portfolio = $400 + $800 = $1,200
Percentage of A in portfolio = $400 / $1,200 = 33.33%
Percentage of B in portfolio = $800 / $1,200 = 66.67%

$$Expected\ Return = (r_1 \times i_1) + (r_n \times i_n)$$

$$7.5\% = (.3333 \times .05) + (.6667 \times x)$$

Expected Return for Stock B = 8.75%

INFLATION-ADJUSTED RETURN

Inflation-adjusted returns measure the performance of securities over a given period of time and subtract the **rate of inflation** over that period of time to provide a clearer picture of how the security actually performed. Simple inflation-adjusted returns are calculated by subtracting the rate of inflation from the rate of return of a security. Inflation reduces the purchasing power of money over time; adjusting returns by inflation helps the investor determine how much real purchasing power was gained in the given period of time. This makes inflation-adjusted returns a function of the present value of money. The long-term rate of inflation in the United States is **3 percent**. If an investment returned 2% annually in a long-term portfolio, the inflation-adjusted rate of return was actually negative. This calculation of return helps investors decide which securities are performing well enough to warrant continued investment.

EXAMPLE 1

A portfolio had an annual return of 12%. The inflation rate during that same time period was 2%. Calculate the inflation-adjusted return.

The inflation adjusted return for this portfolio is 9.8%.

EXAMPLE 2

A portfolio returned 17% during a given year. The inflation adjusted return calculated for the portfolio was 12%. Calculate the inflation rate for this time period.

Inflation rate = x = 4.46%

After-Tax Return

After-tax return is a measurement of an asset's performance after all **applicable taxes are paid** on the investment. This provides the investor with a means by which more thorough analysis of the performance of the investor's holdings may be performed. Taxes reduce the effective return of securities because of the loss of capital required to pay taxes owed. Simple after-tax returns are calculated by subtracting the tax rate imposed on the gains provided by the security from the rate of return on the security. After-tax returns are helpful in determining the real rates of return. They also provide a unique look at tax-advantaged investments. An investment, such as a municipal bond, is tax-free by state and federal law. A municipal bond that returns 5 percent, then, can actually provide more return than a corporate bond that returns 7 percent, as the after-tax return for the corporate bond can result in a significant decrease.

Example 1

An investor in the 35% federal tax bracket has a portfolio that had the following returns in for 2015:

$700 stock dividends
$300 corporate bond interest

Calculate his after-tax return.

After=tax return = $650

Example 2

An investor in the 35% federal tax bracket has a portfolio that had the following returns in for 2015:

$500 stock dividends
$300 corporate bond interest
$250 municipal bond interest

Calculate his after-tax return.

After=tax return = $770

The municipal bond income is tax-free, so only the dividend and corporate bond income is subjected to the 35% tax rate.

Yield-to-Maturity

Yield-to-maturity measures the yield that would be gained if a bond or other fixed income security were held by an investor until the date at which it **matured**. Yield-to-maturity is calculated using the par value of the security, the current market price, time to maturity, and coupon interest rate paid. If a bond is purchased at a discount, the yield-to-maturity is greater than the current yield or coupon of the bond. If the bond was purchased at a premium, yield-to-maturity would be less than the current yield or coupon. Yield-to-maturity is important to investors seeking current income as it helps them determine if the income that they will receive from a certain security is worth the capital outlay. A bond paying a high coupon that is purchased at a high premium may actually yield less than a bond that sells at a discount but pays a lower coupon.

Current Yield

Current yield is a measurement of the interest or dividends a given security pays compared to the price at which that security is sold. Most often a function of bond and fixed income securities, current yield is calculated by dividing the annual cash flows, or coupon rates in the case of bonds, by the market price of the security. A bond selling at a **discount** provides a higher yield than the coupon rate. A bond selling at a **premium** provides a lower yield on investment than the coupon rate. Current yield is an important factor of consideration for those investors seeking income from their portfolios. It allows the investor to determine if the amount of income that they would receive from a potential investment is worth the initial capital outlay or if the capital could be invested to great effect in another investment.

BENCHMARK PORTFOLIOS

Benchmark portfolios are portfolios designed to mimic the **volatility** of the benchmark they purport to track. As an example, a portfolio benchmarked to the Dow Jones Industrial Average would reasonably be expected to rise 10 percent if the Dow Jones rose 10 percent. The same applies to other benchmarks such as the S&P 500 or the Russell 2000. Benchmark portfolios are often viewed as a product of the efficient market theory, the theory that it is impossible to outperform the market. Benchmarked portfolios are often less expensive to manage and less expensive for investors to participate therein. This is because once the portfolio is indexed to the benchmark, little to no additional cost associated with investment management is incurred. Managers who actively manage portfolios often incur large expenses and pass them on to investors. This is usually not the case with benchmarked portfolios.

Client Investment Recommendations and Strategies Chapter Quiz

1. Which form of business ownership provides the least amount of liability protection?

a. Limited Liability Partnership
b. The S Corporation
c. Sole proprietorship
d. Limited Liability Corporation

2. For a 29-year-old single client, with a high risk tolerance, low tax bracket, and $50,000 in savings, we can eliminate what asset class from our recommendation?

a. Money market funds
b. Municipal bond funds
c. Emerging market stock funds
d. Individual dividend paying stocks

3. For a 60-year-old woman with a low risk tolerance, no investing experience, five years until retirement, and only $50,000 in savings; which investment can we eliminate from recommending?

a. Bond mutual fund
b. Growth and income mutual fund
c. Individual small cap stocks
d. Money market funds

4. Which is not an appropriate method of diversification for a mutual fund?

a. Industry diversification
b. Geographic diversification
c. Demographic diversification
d. Market cap diversification

5. The "efficient frontier" is most closely associated with what?

a. The efficient market hypothesis
b. The CAPM
c. Asset allocation
d. Modern portfolio theory

6. Someone who diversifies across sectors, asset classes, styles and then meticulously rebalances every 12 months is said to be practicing:

a. Strategic asset allocation
b. Tactical asset allocation
c. Sector rotation
d. Dollar cost averaging

7. The biggest advantage of a Roth IRA is:

a. Tax deferral of gains
b. Tax deductibility of contribution
c. Tax free withdrawals
d. Cheaper investment options through group plan

8. Which retirement plan cannot be set up by an S corporation for its employees?

a. SEP IRA
b. Safe Harbor 401k
c. Keogh plan
d. ESOP plan

9. Which of the following can you not purchase on margin inside an UTMA account?

a. NYSE stocks
b. Options
c. OTC securities on FRB's approved list
d. None of the above

10. Which type of account is most likely to simply and inexpensively avoid probate?

a. Joint ownership with Rights of Survivorship
b. Pay-on-Death account
c. Joint ownership with Tenancy in Common
d. Single ownership with a beneficiary

Client Investment Recommendations and Strategies Chapter Quiz Answers

1. C: The sole proprietorship offers the owner no additional liability protection, unlike all three other business structures.

2. B: With a low tax bracket and a long time horizon, muni bonds can be eliminated from this group.

3. C: With a low risk tolerance and a short time horizon, individual small caps should be eliminated from consideration.

4. C: Demographics applies to people, not stocks.

5. D: Modern portfolio theory is used to try and create a portfolio that resides on the efficient frontier, where the optimum balance of risk and return is obtained.

6. A: This is straightforward strategic asset allocation methodology in action.

7. C: The Roth allows the investor to withdraw all money, both contributions and gains, tax free in retirement. There are also special provisions where you can withdraw before retirement age for a down payment on a first house, for example.

8. C: Keogh plans may only be set up for sole proprietorship companies, and contributions are allowed as a % of self-employment income.

9. D: UTMA/UGMA accounts cannot be set up on margin. They are fiduciary accounts, and margin increases risk.

10. B: The pay-on-death account is designed to avoid probate and be transferred directly to beneficiary upon the death of the account owner.

Laws, Regulations, and Guidelines, including Prohibition on Unethical Business Practices

Regulation of Investment Advisers, Including State-Registered and Federal Covered Advisers

INVESTMENT ADVISOR

The **Investment Advisers Act of 1940** provided a legal definition for the *investment advisor* designation and required advisors to register with the **Securities and Exchange Commission (SEC)**. According to the act, an investment advisor is a person (legal or natural) who "provides investment advice, reports, or analyses with respect to securities, is in the business of providing advice or analyses, and receives compensation, directly or indirectly, for these services." The stock market crash of 1929 brought sweeping reform to the securities industry. The Investment Advisers Act of 1940 was passed to reduce fraud perpetrated upon investors. The principal goals of the Investment Advisers Act of 1940 were to provide for the regulation of individuals and corporations in the business of distributing investment advice and to institute the standard of ethics for the industry.

UNIFORM SECURITIES ACT

The **Uniform Securities Act** is a legislative attempt to bring uniformity to state securities laws that are widely varied, also known as **blue-sky laws**. The Uniform Securities Act, or **USA**, outlines civil and criminal liabilities for abuse of the uniform laws. Each state's securities laws are overseen by an administrator. The administrator, or the office of the administrator, has jurisdiction of all activities that occur in the state concerning the securities industry. The blue-sky laws not only bring uniformity to multiple states' laws but also provides for consumer investor protection. Many terms that are often unclear to unsophisticated investors are defined under the Uniform Securities Act, helping those investors make more-informed decisions.

REGISTRATION PROCESS AND NOTICE-FILING REQUIREMENTS

Investment advisors must submit to a **registration process** as set forth in the Uniformed Securities Act. Although the application process may vary from state to state, the registration process usually takes on the same basic form. Applicants must make an application to the state administrator, supply a consent to service of process, which allows clients to file legal complaints, pay any fees associated with filing for application, post any bonds that may be made mandatory by the administrator, and pass any tests or examinations as required. Dependent upon the requirements of the administrator, investment advisor applicants must provide the following information to the Securities Exchange Commission (SEC) via **notice-filing**: registration statements on file with the SEC, amendments made to those registration statements, the amount of value of securities offered in each state, and consent to service of process.

REQUIREMENTS AFTER REGISTRATION

Following the registration of an investment advisor, the Securities Exchange Commission requires that detailed **records** be kept, including a journal of transactions of cash in and disbursement out; ledgers detailing any expense, liability, reserve, asset, capital, or income accounts; documentation of orders placed by the advisor and any modifications thereto; financial records, bills and statements, original copies of written communication, and records of accounts with discretionary designations; any powers of attorney held by the investment advisor; written contracts; copies of all advertisements; and records of securities transactions in which the investment advisor has some amount of ownership. These records must be maintained in a secure location for five years. After the first two years, the oldest three years may be digitized and stored on the memory of a computer. The records should not be accessible to the public but should be readily available should the administrator choose to audit them.

Exemption Regulations for Exempt Reporting Advisers

While numerous reporting advisers are required to register with the SEC or state regulators, the Dodd-Frank Act amended the Investment Advisers Act of 1940 to create a class of **Exempt Reporting Advisers** (ERAs). These advisers still have certain reporting duties but are not required to register with the SEC or state regulators. The exemptions governing ERAs can be split into two categories. The **private fund adviser exemption** allows advisers with only private funds and with <$150 million in assets under management (AUM) to qualify as ERAs. The **venture capital adviser exemption** allows advisers of only venture capital funds to qualify as ERAs; this exemption applies regardless of any AUM limit.

Investment Adviser Representatives

Whereas **investment advisers (IAs)** are any person, group, or company who analyzes or recommends securities for a profit, **investment adviser representatives (IARs)** are individual persons (ordinarily employees) of an IA who either provide investment services or supervise those who do. (For instance, by this definition, an employee who solicits investments for an IA would be an IAR, but a merely clerical employee for an IA would not.) IARs must individually register with the state, beyond the registration requirements for IAs.

The **Investment Advisers Act of 1940** requires the supervision of IARs for all IAs registered with the SEC. In particular, this regulation requires IAs to appoint a Chief Compliance Officer (CCO) whose responsibility it is to know, apply, and report on his firm's policies and procedures concerning regulatory compliance, including answering any questions asked about particular supervised persons.

Regulation of Investment Adviser Representatives

Investment Advisor Representative

According to the SEC, an **investment advisor representative** (**IAR** for short) is an individual who is under the supervision of an investment advisor. In order to qualify as an investment advisor representative, rather than fall into the category of an investment advisor, certain limitations on the capacity of the individual must be in effect, including the following:

- The individual must have **more than five clients** who are considered natural persons (i.e., not businesses, trusts, or other entities which do not qualify for natural person status). In addition, the clients that fall into this category must make up at least 10% of the IAR's client base.
- The individual must **communicate** with the clients of the investment advisor.
- The individual cannot provide **impersonal investment advice**, meaning that the individual may only provide recommendations if they meet the underlying objective of the specific client.

Regulation of Broker-Dealers

Brokers and Dealers

A **broker** is a person or institution which acts as a **middleman** between the buyer of a security and the seller of a security. The broker makes his profit by charging a sales charge, or commission, for arranging the transaction. Brokers do not own any products for which they arrange transactions, but simply facilitate the transfer of ownership from a seller to a buyer.

A **dealer** is a person or institution which sells its own inventory to buyers (like a used-car dealer). A dealer charges a **markdown** when he purchases inventory, lowering the price he pays for the inventory; and he charges a **markup** when he sells it, increasing the price the customer pays for it. Furthermore, dealers sometimes intend for the inventory to appreciate in value while they hold it.

Whether a firm is acting in the capacity of a broker or dealer must be disclosed on the receipt of trade, or the confirmation. Commissions need to be disclosed, but not necessarily markups or markdowns.

Firms are prohibited from acting as both a broker and a dealer in the same transaction. Either a commission can be charged, or a markup or markdown, but not both.

Broker-Dealer

Broker-dealers are any person or persons, natural or legal, who transact securities business on their own behalf and for the benefit of others. Broker-dealers trading for their own accounts act as dealers, and when acting on behalf of others in an agency capacity, they are brokers. The dual nature of the business led to the creation of the name **broker-dealer**. Per the Uniform Securities Act, all broker-dealers must register with state administration in the states in which the broker-dealer practices business in addition to the Securities Exchange Commission, or the SEC. This is usually accomplished by submitting an SEC Form B/D that has been adapted to suit the states' requirements.

Requirements After Registration

After broker-dealers have completed registration, they must continue to comply with **state and federal securities laws**. The state may impose capital requirements upon the broker-dealer. These requirements are called **net capital requirements** and require the broker to retain a certain amount of liquid assets. Further, the administrator may require that the broker-dealer maintain surety bonds, bonds by which a third party guarantees the broker dealer will honor all obligations owed to clients if they have discretionary power or custody of a client's funds. The amounts or denominations of the net capital requirements and the surety bonds required by the state administrator may not exceed the limits set forth by the Securities Exchange Commission. Broker-dealers must keep **records** pertaining to accounts, memoranda, blotters, and so on, as required by regulations established by the administrator. These records should be retained for at least three years.

Regulation of Agents of Broker-Dealers

Registration Process of Agents of Broker-Dealers

A person who is registering to be an **agent of a broker-dealer** must submit an application. This is **Form U-4** in most cases. Without exception, the Uniform Securities Act requires that all persons transacting securities-related business must be **registered** in the state in which that person does business. There is no minimum net worth requirement for an agent. Although there is no net worth requirement, the Administrator may require that the agent be bonded. While agents are waiting for their registration to become effective, they may act in any capacity that does not require them to contact clients or solicit securities transactions. They may act in a ministerial role and perform clerical and administrative duties.

Regulation of Securities and Issuers

Securities and Issuers

The technical definition of the term **security** as defined in the Uniform Securities Act (USA) has an important distinction. The reason for this is that the regulations outlined in the USA only apply to securities as defined in the USA. The definition of security as outlined by the USA is an investment of capital assets in a common enterprise with the anticipation of growing returns resulting mostly from the energies of a person separate from the investor. An **issuer**, as defined under the USA, is a person who issues or proposes the issue of a given security. Issuers are generally governments or companies. The forms of government issuing securities range from the federal to the municipal level.

Preliminary Prospectus and Final Prospectus

The **preliminary prospectus** must be submitted along with the registration statement for the issuance of new securities, as the preliminary prospectus is required to be available to potential investors during the cooling-off period. This prospectus includes the general but important facts regarding the securities issuance, but does not include the public offering price or the date when the issue will first be sold. Preliminary prospectuses are also called red herrings because they include a statement in red lettering on the cover declaring that they are preliminary, and thus that some items might be subject to change.

The **final prospectus** is prepared near the end of the cooling-off period. It includes the public offering price, as well as the underwriter spread and the date when the securities will be available (the delivery date).

Prospectus Filing Requirements Found in SEC Rule 430, 430A, and 430B

Prospectus for use prior to effective date (Rule 430) - prospectus can be used prior to effective date so long as all requirements are met.

Prospectus in a registration statement at time of effectiveness (Rule 430A) - a prospectus submitted as part of a registration statement can omit certain details so long as certain requirements are met, such as the securities only being offered for cash.

Prospectus in a registration statement after effective date (Rule 430B) - a prospectus filed with a registration statement can omit certain unknown or unavailable information.

Registration of Securities

The **registration of securities** in compliance with the USA may be accomplished in a number of ways. The three ways securities may be registered under the USA are by notice filing, qualification, and coordination. **Notice filing** occurs when the issuer provides documents from the Securities Exchange Commission (SEC) filing to the administrator. Notice filing requires documents filed with their SEC registration statements, amendments thereto, a relevant valuation of the securities, and consent to service of process. Registration by **coordination** occurs after the administrator is supplied with prospectuses in compliance with the Securities Act of 1933, the issuer's articles of incorporation, bylaws, and the underwriting agreement. The administrator may also require other info filed relating to the Act of 1933. Any amendments to the security must be filed thereafter. Registration by **qualification** occurs when the issuer submits to an application process that includes information regarding the business and the nature thereof, detailed financial statements of the issuer, type of security offered and how the proceeds will be used, submission of prospectus, and a copy of the security with an opinion of legality according to legal counsel.

Post Registration Requirements

After the registration of a nonexempt security, the administrator has the authority to demand that any **amendments** to the security be submitted in a timely fashion to ensure the maintenance of valid and relevant information regarding the new issuance of the security. The registration of the newly issued security is valid for one year after the date of issuance. If additional shares are issued without significant changes to the security within that period of time, a new registration is unnecessary. New issues of the security must retain an identical public offering price to the original issue, and the compensation that the underwriters are given must remain identical to that of the primary registration statement. The administrator must be notified immediately of any significant changes to the security issue to retain legal registration of the issue.

Exemptions from Security Registration

An **exempt security** is exempt due to the nature of the issuer. Securities issued by United States governments and Canadian governments, and guaranteed by those governments, are **exempt from registration** under the Uniform Securities Act (USA). Any security issued and guaranteed by a foreign government that retains a diplomatic status with the United States is also exempt from registration under the USA. They are exempt from registration due to the relationship foreign governments have with the United States and the presumed trustworthiness of those governments. Other exempt securities include those securities that are issued and guaranteed by depository institutions that are federally chartered or authorized to transact business in a given state; securities issued and guaranteed by insurance companies; public utility securities issued by the utilities holding company; federally covered securities such as rights, warrants, debt securities, and preferred stock; nonprofit security issues; employee benefit plans that issue securities; and specific money market issues, the most common of which are commercial paper and banker's acceptances. While the preceding are exempt from registration, no security is exempt from the antifraud clauses of the USA.

Remedies and Administrative Provisions

Authority of the Administrator

As clearly defined in the Uniform Securities Act (USA), the **jurisdiction and authority** granted to the administrator apply only to securities transactions that were initiated in the administrator's state of authority, directed to that administrator's state of authority, or accepted in that state. According to the USA, the administrator may use any of **four powers** in the enforcement of its regulations: make, change, or repeal rules and orders; conduct investigations and issue subpoenas; issue cease and desist orders and seek injunctions; and deny, suspend, cancel, or revoke registrations and licenses. As a result of the administrator having access to the powers outlined above, the administrator is under a moral imperative to act honestly and not receive any benefit from the use of these powers or nonpublic information to which he or she may be privy because of his or her official duty.

ADMINISTRATIVE ACTION IN ENFORCING A STATE'S SECURITIES LAWS

The **administrator** has certain powers to ensure that the Uniform Securities Act (USA) is followed. The administrator has the power to create, change, and repeal existing rules, orders, and forms in the execution of the **USA's policies**. While rules and orders created by the administrator carry the same weight as those in the USA, they are not considered part of the USA. Rules and orders differ in that rules apply to all persons falling under the jurisdiction of the administrator, and an order applies to only one occurrence or person. The administrator has the power to conduct investigations and issue subpoenas in the investigation of accusations of improper conduct. To assist in the execution of the investigation, the administrator may require sworn statements in relation to the matter, publish facts and circumstances surrounding the subject, subpoena witnesses and require their presence and testimony, and take relevant evidence and demand records regarding the issue. The administrator may also issue cease and desist orders to prevent further violations from occurring. If the administrator finds that it is in the public interest to do so, he or she may deny, suspend, cancel, or revoke registrations.

PENALTIES AND LIABILITIES OUTSIDE THE STATE ADMINISTRATOR'S JURISDICTION

The Uniform Securities Act (USA) allows for **criminal and civil penalties** for those persons abusing the regulations. Clients are also protected from financial loss resultant from the illegal sale of securities or offering of investment advice. The investment advisor may be subject to civil liabilities under the USA if an illegal sale of security was made, material facts were not disclosed at the time of investment advice, the advisor is part of a suit against a broker-dealer, the broker was not registered under the USA, or the sale of the investments were in violation of rules and orders of the administrator. Those parties guilty of fraud perpetrated in the execution of a securities transaction may be subject to criminal penalties. If convicted, the offending party is subject to up to $5,000 in fines and/or three years in jail. Jail time is only possible if the offending party was aware of the law he or she infracted.

Communication with Clients and Prospects

PROPER DISCLOSURES TO MAINTAIN PROPER ETHICAL CONDUCT

Full and proper disclosure is one of the keys to investment advisors maintaining ethical practices. Full disclosure to the client provides an amount of transparency that helps the client make informed decisions about the actions they may or may not choose to take with their funds. Disclosures made to clients to help them make these decisions are wide ranging and varied. Such disclosures include the charging of fees and commissions to the account, potential conflicts of interest that may arise, and agency-cross transactions. These disclosures help the client make informed decisions, such as providing a reason why an advisor may make a particular suggestion. Investors should also receive full disclosure of risk and be informed that securities transactions are not guaranteed and may result in loss. They should be fully aware that securities transactions are not covered by the Federal Deposit Insurance Corporation (FDIC) and that there is no bank guarantee.

DELIVERY OF ANNUAL REPORTS AND NOTICES OF CORPORATE ACTIONS

A broker is responsible for informing his customer of various actions taken by corporations in which the customer has some share or interest. This includes notifying the customer about **annual reports** for the corporation (as well as interim reports, if necessary) and notices of various corporate actions. If a corporation has split its stock, tendered new stock, established some kind of shareholder voting by proxy, announced plans to repurchase stock, or done some other action which is worthy of the customer's attention, the broker should seek to **notify** him.

REQUIRED DISCLOSURES FOR SPECIFIC TRANSACTIONS

Offering documents are disclosures provided by issuers of securities providing specific and detailed financial information concerning both the issuer and the offering itself.

Prospectuses are formal documents which brokers are legally required to file with the SEC. They provide information about investments being offered for sale to the public, giving information so that investors can make intelligent and informed decisions. Stocks and bonds have two types of prospectuses, preliminary and final.

Red herrings are preliminary prospectuses. They are called such, not because they are misleading (as are "red herrings" in logic and rhetoric), but because they include a statement in red lettering on the cover declaring that they are preliminary, and thus that some items might be subject to change.

Statements of additional information, sometimes abbreviated as SAIs, are supplementary documents which are added to prospectuses for mutual fund offerings. These statements provide further details on the fund, although they are not strictly necessary for investors to make informed decisions, and therefore they are not legally required by fund companies to include. (However, they must provide such information for free to customers upon request.)

Material events are any events which substantively impact a prospective investor's decision to invest or not. These can be economic events, political events, or anything else. Brokers should be aware of these and report them to customers as is appropriate.

In order to avoid conflicts of interest and thereby protect customers, brokers are required to disclose any **control relationships** they have with the issuer of securities, bonds in particular. Although the initial disclosure can be merely verbal, before a transaction actually goes through, the customer must be informed in writing of the control issue. This usually takes place at confirmation.

UNLAWFUL REPRESENTATION OF A SECURITY REGARDING REGISTRATION

The registration of a security with government agencies does not imply its approval of the issue and does not imply any type of **guarantee of performance**. The registration of a security with the correct agency means only that the registration process was completed. To imply or to allow a client to think that government registration somehow implies a Securities Exchange Commission (SEC) stamp of approval and recommendation is unethical and illegal. The advisor should be certain that the client understand that registration of securities means only that securities are registered. As such, the advisor should not use language such as *SEC approved* and *good offering.* If the advisor wishes to inform the client that the issue has been registered with the proper agencies, proper handling would be to tell the client that the security has been *registered* with the SEC.

PERFORMANCE GUARANTEES

A **performance guarantee** is a guarantee against **loss** issued by an advisor or some other broker. Performance guarantees may be verbal and explicit in nature or subtle and implicit to avoid legal situations. While an outright verbal or written guarantee of performance may be the easiest to identify, there are many types of performance guarantees. One way of guaranteeing against loss is for an advisor to share in the losses of a client's account in a greater proportion than that advisor has assets in the account. Advisors or brokers may also present large gifts to the client to compensate for losses incurred. Both of the preceding are performance guarantees that are illegal and unethical. Guarantees of performance are unethical because they are not a reflection of reality and mislead the client. Performance guarantees in all forms are **illegal and unethical** except in the case of **insurance contracts** such as variable life annuities and universal life insurance.

Client Contracts

The **business relationship** between the client and advisor is outlined in the **contract** between the client and advisor. The Uniform Securities Act (USA) requires that all investment advisory contracts be in writing, while federal regulations only stipulate that the contract be oral. Another difference between the USA and federal regulations is the fair assessment of fees. The USA dictates that fees must be competitive, while federal regulations only require that they be reasonable for services offered. To maintain an ethical and transparent contract, the contract should outline the services offered, terms of the contract, the advisory fees charged, the amount of any prepaid fees to be refunded at contract termination, if there is discretionary authority given to the advisor, the fact that the contract may not be assigned without client authorization, and if the advisor is structured as a partnership, that the advisor notify the client if a change is made in minority interest.

Advertising Limitations

The Uniform Securities Act includes specific **limitations** regarding the permissible contents of **advertisements** for investment advisers.

Advertisements are classified as a message about the investment adviser that is directed to more than one person. Investment adviser advertisements may not include testimonials of any kind. If the advertisement contains any information regarding the historical performance of the securities recommended by the investment adviser, the advertisement may not limit the information to successful recommendations. Instead, if the advertisement references the performance of a particular recommended stock, the advertisement must reference the performance of all of the recommendations the investment adviser made regarding the same type of securities over that previous year (or longer). If historical performance is referenced, the advertisement must accurately reflect recommendations resulting in losses as well as those resulting in gains.

All these limitations apply to advertising regardless of medium, hence applying equally to physical correspondence, email, social media, and so forth.

Ethical Practices and Fiduciary Obligations

Charging of Fees to Clients' Accounts

According to the Uniform Securities Act (USA), **fees** charged to a client's account must be competitive with those fees charged by other firms for similar services. Federal regulations, however, only require that the fees must be reasonable for the services rendered. To maintain an ethical practice, the advisor should disclose the amount of the fee charged for advisory services or the formula used to calculate the fee. The formula for fee calculation is usually a simple calculation as a percentage of assets under management. An important concept to remember is the waiver of fees due to poor performance in an account amounts to a performance guarantee and is therefore illegal. Performance-based fees are generally prohibited by the USA but are allowed under certain exceptions.

Charging of Commissions to Clients' Accounts

Charging commissions to a client's account is an acceptable practice if the amount of commission is **disclosed** to the investor before the commission is charged. Commissions are not typically applied to transactions originating from an account that is covered by an advisory contract. Commissions charged should be fair and not take advantage of a lack of knowledge on the client's part. The advisor should also understand the intricacies of collecting commissions from both parties in an agency-cross transaction. When the advisor acts in the role of a broker in an agency-cross transaction, he or she will collect commissions from both parties in the transaction. To maintain ethical practices, the advisor should clearly disclose to both parties that he or she will be receiving commissions from both parties.

Charging of Performance-Based Fees to Clients' Accounts

Performance-based fees are investment advisory fees that are calculated based on the advisor collecting a **share of the capital appreciation** that occurs in the advised party's account. Fees charged based upon the total amount of assets managed are not performance-based fees. Performance-based fees are only charged to high net-worth clients. While the advisor may share in the gains of the account, the gains must be netted against the losses as well. Hedge funds commonly use performance-based fees as a means of collecting compensation. As long as all applicable laws and regulations are followed, charging performance-based fees is completely ethical and legal, assuming proper disclosure to and consent from the client.

Soft Dollars

Soft dollars are payments made to brokerages for services rendered by promising to trade through that brokerage, thus providing that brokerage with large amounts of **commissions**. Services rendered in such situations are typically research solicited from the brokerage by an investment company, such as a mutual fund. Full disclosure of this arrangement to clients is needed to maintain the legality of such issues. Many view soft dollar arrangements as an ethical gray area. Despite its legality, many view soft dollar arrangements as unethical because the investment company is effectively paying for services from the accounts of the clients because the money that the brokerage receives comes from the commissions they charge.

Penny Stock Rules

Disclosure of compensation to brokers or dealers (SEC Rule 15g-4) - a broker/dealer must disclose to the customer the total compensation received in connection with transaction before transacting in penny stock on behalf of the customer.

Disclosure of compensation of associated persons in connection with penny stock transactions (SEC Rule 15g-5) - a broker/dealer must disclose to the customer the total compensation received by any associated person of the broker/dealer in connection with the transaction before transacting in penny stock on behalf of the customer.

Custody of a Client's Funds

The term **custody**, as it relates to securities, describes **holding**, whether directly or indirectly, the funds and securities of another person or possessing authority to acquire those funds. Safekeeping of custodial funds as required by the Investment Advisor Act of 1940 requires the advisor to have a qualified custodian to hold the assets of the client in distinct accounts, the client must be aware that their funds are being held by the custodian, and regular statements of account must be delivered to the client by the custodian or the advisor. Advisors in possession of client funds must act in the utmost confidence of the client and for the client's best interest, not out of desire for personal gain.

Discretion over a Client's Funds

Having **discretion** over a client's funds gives the advisor **authority** to decide which security to trade, whether to buy or sell that security, and the amount of that security. These conditions are commonly referred to as the **three A's**. Respective to the sentence above, the three A's are *asset*, *action*, and *amount*. When an advisor accepts discretion over a client's account, he or she is ethically bound to act in a fiduciary manner regarding the client's funds, that is, in the best interest of the client at all times and not for personal gain. Discretion over assets is granted through a written trade authorization documented or via a limited power of attorney. The advisor with discretion must constantly adhere to the following guidelines: All discretionary transactions executed must be clearly labeled as such, records of all discretionary transactions must be kept, and an officer or a principal of the advisory firm is required to authorize the transaction in writing.

Trading Authorization

Trading authorization usually occurs in accounts that require a custodian and accounts that require an advisor to act in a fiduciary role. Securities contained in these types of accounts, such as an account covered by the Uniform Transfer to Minors Act, require someone other than the owner to execute trades. Trading authorization is usually obtained in one of two ways: through a **limited trade authorization document** or through a **power of attorney document**. Furthermore, there are two types of powers of attorney to grant access to the account. A full power of attorney will allow the authorized trader to deposit and withdraw securities and funds and make decisions about investments for the owner. A limited power of attorney limits the authority the advisor has. This limit of powers is outlined in the power of attorney document.

Prudent Investor Standards

Prudent investor standards require that an advisor in a fiduciary role behave as if the assets over which that advisor has responsibility were his or her **own assets**. These prudent standards insist that all aspects of the client's needs should be considered and that the investments not be excessively volatile and prone to unreasonable amounts of risk. Prudent investing standards do not always result in high performance or even reach the goal of the investor, however. Prudent investing applies to the means by which the investment decision is reached. It is always possible to follow prudent investing standards, while it may not always be possible that those prudent decisions end up with desirable results.

Suitability

The term **suitability**, as it applies to investing, refers to the act of determining the client's **needs** and applying those needs in the consideration of securities best suited to those needs. Clients in need of current income and capital preservation will not benefit from the purchase of common stock of risky companies with small-market capitalization (small cap). The common stock of small-cap companies does not typically pay dividends, resulting in no income, and they are volatile, working against the need of capital preservation. Conversely, a young investor whose goal is capital appreciation and has the ability to absorb and recover from losses would not be suited to fixed income securities. The younger investor has no need of income from his or her investments, and the stability of the investments detracts from the goal of capital appreciation. Common stock of small-cap companies is more suited to the younger investor's needs. Also of consideration when determining suitability is the investor's risk appetite. A younger investor may not be able to accept large swings in his or her portfolio, thereby requiring a more conservative strategy than other investors of similar demographics.

Bank Secrecy Act

The **Bank Secrecy Act (BSA)** is also known as the Currency and Foreign Transactions Reporting Act.

The BSA is federal legislation that targets broker-dealers and financial dealers that may be aiding clients attempting to launder money, evade taxes, or engage in other criminal behavior.

The BSA instituted record-keeping requirements for certain cash purchases. In addition, the BSA requires broker-dealers and financial institutions to report any suspicious activities that indicate a potential attempt to launder money, evade taxes, or engage in other illegal activities. The BSA also instituted an obligation for financial institutions and broker-dealers to report any aggregate daily cash transaction in excess of ten thousand dollars.

The goal of the BSA is to detect current **violations** and to prevent future **illegal activity**. The USA Patriot Act established additional requirements designed to prevent the laundering of money by terrorist groups.

Indications of Possible Money Laundering Activity

Securities dealers are obligated to **report** activity that could be tied to money laundering. The industry has identified four red flags that point to suspicious activity that should be reported.

1. If the broker-dealer knows that money involved in the transaction is the **result of criminal activity** or that the transaction is intended to disguise illegal activity, the transaction must be reported.
2. If the broker-dealer would be required to **engage in criminal activity** in order to complete a requested transaction, it must be reported.
3. If the broker-dealer is aware that the purpose of the transaction is to **circumvent the provisions of the Bank Secrecy Act**, the transaction must be reported.
4. The last red flag requires the broker-dealer to consider the purpose that will be served by the transaction. If the broker-dealer cannot identify a **legitimate purpose** for a particular transaction based on available facts, the transaction should be reported as suspicious.

Maintaining Custody of Clients' Assets

Investment advisers may only maintain possession or control of their client's assets under specific circumstances. Such possession or control is referred to as **maintaining custody** of the assets. Investment advisers may not maintain custody of their client's funds if the Administrator has issued a rule prohibiting such custody.

If the Administrator has not ruled to prohibit custody, the investment adviser is obligated to inform the Administrator any time the investment adviser has custody of its client's assets. Investment advisers that maintain custody of their clients' assets are required to provide regular statements to their custodial clients that outline the value of the account, account transactions, and the location of all of the clients' assets. At a minimum, investment advisers must provide these statements to custodial clients on quarterly basis.

Outside Business Activities and Outside Securities Accounts of Registered Individuals

The **Financial Industry Regulatory Authority (FINRA)** requires that registered persons **notify** their employing FINRA member if they are compensated in any form by another party for any activities performed other than investment-related activities. The employing FINRA member must then approve or disapprove the activity. If the activity would create a conflict of interest with the firm's customers or be potentially illegal or hazardous to the FINRA member's well-being, they will disallow the activity. Passive investment activities on the part of registered individuals do not require disclosure, although investment accounts held with another FINRA member must be disclosed to their employing FINRA firm.

Providing Loans to or Accepting Loans from Clients

Loaning money to a client is not an acceptable or ethical practice unless the investment advisor is in the business of loaning money or the client to whom the money is being loaned is a business affiliate of the advisor. Loaning funds to clients creates a **conflict of interest** due to the fact that the client is now also a debtor to the advisor. Such relationships can affect the decisions advisors make regarding the client's funds. Conversely, advisors should not accept loans from clients unless the client is a financial institution practicing the business of making loans. Advisors have access to large of amounts of personal information about the client. When advisors use this information to their advantage by soliciting loans, they have perpetrated a breach of confidentiality with the client that could create a conflict of interest.

Sharing in Profits and Losses in a Client's Account

Advisors may share in the **profits and losses** in a client's account so long as those profits and losses are **proportional** to the advisors' share of the investment made. Ethical issues are implied when an advisor accepts a larger portion of the loss than his or her share based on the amount of investment the advisor made. The advisor may accept a larger portion of the loss to entice the client to use his or her services. This practice is effectively guaranteeing against a loss, which is both illegal and unethical. The ethical issues that arise from an advisor accepting more than his or her contributed allocation of profits from a shared account are based upon charging and accepting unreasonable compensation.

Client Confidentiality

The level of **client confidentiality** that must be maintained can best be described as **absolute**. Only people directly involved in the servicing of the client and the client's accounts should have knowledge as to who the client is and the client's personal information. Those persons servicing the accounts should only access the client's accounts to service it, and not for any other reason. The **Graham-Leach Bliley Act** is the congressional act that mandates that all financial institutions keep client information secure. This information includes, but is not limited to, private information such as Social Security numbers, account numbers, and annual income. The Graham-Leach Bliley Act also provides for the negligent or inadvertent disclosure of personal information, such as leaving a tax return in an area that is accessible by non-servicing personnel.

Insider Trading

Insider trading refers to a person or persons trading a specific security to prevent loss or generate gain based on that person or those persons' access to **nonpublic information** that is relevant to the security. Insider trading is illegal and unethical because this gives those with knowledge inside the company an unfair advantage over those investors on the outside of the company. While directors of companies and company planners may have the most direct access to material nonpublic information, they are not the only parties able to trade on inside information. Family members of persons with nonpublic information may also illegally practice insider trading. Insider trading is always illegal and unethical as long as it is done with nonpublic information. After the information has become public, trading on the information, even if practiced by insiders, is perfectly legal.

Selling Away

Selling away is the act of a broker soliciting a client or prospective client to buy securities that are **not offered** by the broker's employer. Selling away is usually a violation of the contract that the broker has with the employer, usually a broker-dealer, and is therefore unethical. Breaches of contract, such as selling away, can lead to a broker-dealer terminating its relationship with a broker. Selling away also usually constitutes a violation of securities regulation and can have legal consequences. The most common reason a broker will sell away is because the security is not a publicly offered security and is a private placement.

Market Manipulation

Market manipulation refers to the manipulation of financial markets by creating **false or inflated prices** for securities. Market manipulation can be accomplished by large investors making an unusually large number of transactions below the current value of a security to purposely create fear that the asset is underperforming and drive down the prices. Alternatively, those who engage in market manipulation may create multiple buy and sell orders for a single security, artificially inflating the volume of trading for the security. Both of these practices can lead to other events that may change the direction of markets to the benefit of those practicing market manipulation. Market manipulation is illegal in the United States and is an unethical practice.

Personal Securities Trading

IAs are required to have a code of ethics which covers **personal securities trading (PST)** by all supervised persons in the company. This specifically applies to **access persons**, that is, persons who have special access to any nonpublic information concerning customers' holdings or transactions, or any other material investment information. The code of ethics must require that IARs report their initial and annual securities holdings—what securities they own upon arriving at the company and every year thereafter—in addition to quarterly reports showing their securities transactions. The IA is then required to review these reports to ensure that no unethical PST is taking place.

Regulations Regarding Political Contributions

The Investment Advisers Act of 1940 prohibits investment advisers from providing their services to any government client for a period of two years following any **political contribution** they have made. And this rule applies not merely to those who make contributions to officials who are elected or to officials who later become elected, but to all officials who *may* become elected. Furthermore, advisers are forbidden from soliciting contributions for various officials or candidates if he is also pursuing or providing business with the government.

Churning

Churning is the act of an advisor making trades in a client's account for the sole purpose of generating **commissions** for the advisor. This is unethical and illegal even in the event that it provides the client with a profit. Advisors have a fiduciary responsibility to act in the client's best interest with the client's money at all times. Churning is not acting in the best interest of the client; rather an advisor practicing churning is acting unethically in the pursuit of profit. The simplest way to avoid churning is for the client to participate in an advised account in which advisors are not paid based on commission, but they are compensated based on a percentage of assets under management charged as a fee. These advised accounts are called fee-based accounts.

Reverse Churning

Reverse churning occurs when a client enters a **fee-based relationship** with an advisor but regular purchases are not made for the client. When a client enters a fee-based relationship, it is to help reduce the costs the client pays associated with commission paid to the advisor. A client in a fee-based relationship that is not receiving a benefit by having commissions waived on normal security purchases is paying fees he or she wouldn't have to pay in a commission-based account. This is effectively reverse churning as the client is paying more than necessary for the same benefit received. Fee-based accounts are attractive for advisors and clients as they keep fees low for the client and establish a relationship that benefits the advisor. This may appear to be the best option in all cases, but if the advisor believes a buy-and-hold strategy is best for the client, the advisor may inadvertently practice reverse churning.

Investment Adviser's Cybersecurity Duties

Investment advisers have strong **fiduciary duties** to protect the sensitive customer information and data which they hold in custody. In our age of increasingly complex and elaborate technology, this duty naturally extends to considerations of **cybersecurity**. Accordingly, investment advisers ought to implement best practices concerning cybersecurity, which can include but is not limited to the following:

- preventing, identifying, and alleviating identity theft
- storing electronic data such that they cannot be rewritten or erased
- adopting policies, procedures, and training pertaining to cybersecurity
- utilizing encrypted or secure servers, emails, and other media as necessary or feasible
- installing antivirus software
- enacting confidentiality agreements with third-party service providers

BC/DR Planning

Though the two terms can be distinguished, **business continuity and disaster recovery (BC/DR) planning** is generally considered as one process by which a firm, in this case a broker-dealer, takes actions to resume the firm's ordinary operations in the case of a significant disrupting event. Plans for these kinds of situation must be in writing, approved by a principal, and include several preventative measures, such as the availability of backup data, alternative communication for a firm with its regulators, customers, and employees, a backup location for employees to work, and a means by which to give customers access to their securities in case of a disaster.

Laws, Regulations, and Guidelines, Including Prohibition on Unethical Business Practices Chapter Quiz

1. Which is not an important issue the NASAA will look at when reviewing Investment Advisers that have custody over client assets?

a. Are clients getting monthly account statements?
b. Is there evidence of excessive trading in the account?
c. Are the assets maintained in segregated accounts?
d. Does the Form ADV reflect the fact that the IA has custody?

2. A state administrator may require a federal covered security to register by notice filing and provide which of the following?

a. All documents filed with their registration statements filed with the SEC
b. Filing fees
c. A consent to service of process
d. All of the above

3. Broker-dealer post registration requirements include all of the following except:

a. Minimum net capital requirements
b. Maintenance of all "books and records"
c. All renewal applications and fees
d. Client communications covered by "attorney-client privilege"

4. The key definition of an agent of a broker-dealer is:

a. Any person who represents an issuer in affecting purchases of securities
b. Any person who represents a BD to affect purchases or sales of securities
c. Any person representing an issuer to affect an exempt transaction
d. Any person who is a BD affecting a purchase or sale of securities

5. Which security is not federally covered, meaning the SEC has not decreed the securities need to be registered with the SEC?

a. A non-profit security
b. An NYSE listed company's bond
c. A NASDAQ listed company's preferred stock
d. Securities issued by a registered Investment Company

6. Which methods of compensation are not allowed for an agent of a broker dealer?

a. Mutual fund 12b-1 fees
b. Markups on bonds
c. Performance based fees
d. Commissions on annuities

7. An adviser with trading authorization over an account, but not custody of that account, must maintain what minimum net capital?

a. Zero
b. A Surety bond for $10,000
c. $10,000
d. $35,000

8. The most serious penalty that might be given for insider trading under the Insider Trading and Securities Fraud Enforcement Act is:

a. Civil penalty up to 100% of profit
b. Revocation of license and civil penalty of 200% of profits
c. Years in federal prison and civil penalties of many times the profit
d. Liability of up to 100% of what "contemporaneous traders" can prove injury

9. Among the criminal penalties and civil liabilities, which of the following is not a remedy available to the Administrator?

a. Four years in prison
b. $5,000 fine
c. Court costs and attorney's fees
d. Price paid for security

10. What would not be involved in a soft dollar arrangement?

a. Computer software
b. Investment research
c. Office equipment discounts
d. Stock bonuses based on growth of accounts

Laws, Regulations, and Guidelines, Including Prohibition on Unethical Business Practices Chapter Quiz Answers

1. A: The NASAA will look that clients receive itemized account statements at least every three months showing the assets and the activity in the account. Monthly statements are not required, although that is the norm.

2. D: Registration by notification with states is mostly an opportunity to collect filing fees for the states. They may require all of the above documents.

3. D: This is a bit of a trick, as broker-dealers do not have communications covered by attorney-client privilege that can be withheld from the Administrator. Generally, BDs are required to retain everything imaginable to do with how they conduct business and it's ALL reviewable by the administrator in the interest of protecting investors.

4. B: The key is a person who is not a BD, who represents a BD or an issuer to effect purchases or sales of securities.

5. A: All non-profit securities are exempt from State registration, but they are not federally covered securities that must be registered with the SEC.

6. C: An agent of a broker dealer is not allowed to be paid through a performance fee arrangement.

7. C: Advisers with custody must maintain $35,000 in minimum net capital, but if they only have discretion and not custody, they are only required to maintain $10,000.

8. C: Insider trading is liable to land you in federal prison on a criminal conviction and will probably also result in a fine of several times the amount of profits; opens up liability to contemporaneous traders; and is guaranteed to result in the loss of registration and the prohibition of future work in the financial industry.

9. A: Criminal penalties can be three years in prison, $5,000 fine, or both. Civil liabilities are in place to effectively make the investor whole.

10. D: Soft dollar arrangements are arrangements between asset managers and broker-dealers, where a good or service that the broker-dealer provides – e.g. computer software, investment research, or office equipment discounts – is compensated not with straight cash (a "hard dollar" arrangement) but with customer commissions. Hence the expenses for such goods or services are harder to trace and less perceptibly passed on to customers, leading some to question the practice.

Series 65 Practice Test

Want to take this practice test in an online interactive format?
Check out the bonus page, which includes interactive practice questions and much more: **https://www.mometrix.com/bonus948/series65**

All of the following are utilized by the "FED" (Federal Reserve Board) to influence the US economy, and specifically, the money supply EXCEPT:

a. raising or reducing the discount rate
b. raising or reducing the reserve requirements for commercial banks
c. purchasing and selling US Treasury securities in the open market
d. raising or reducing the prime rate

2. Which of the following is TRUE of a business cycle pattern?

I. the pattern is impacted by Gross Domestic Product (GDP)
II. just prior to a trough, the economy is in an expansionary phase
III. depression is defined as GDP declining for at least eight consecutive quarters
IV. recession is defined as GDP declining for at least four consecutive quarters

a. I., III., and IV.
b. I. only
c. I. and III.
d. I., II., and IV.

3. A business cycle trough is characterized by:

a. a positive forward outlook for consumer spending to increase
b. a gradual transition for the Gross Domestic Product (GDP) growth rate from a positive to a negative
c. a high rate of inflation
d. low bond prices

4. Which of the following are TRUE of inflation?

I. as inflation increases, bond prices increase, and interest rates fall
II. inflation is characterized as a general economic price increase as measured by an index such as the consumer price index (CPI)
III. excessive demand is one contributing cause of inflation
IV. inflation inertia occurs when the inflation rate is seen to be immediately impacted by changes in the economy

a. I., II., and III.
b. I., III., and IV.
c. II. and III.
d. II. and IV.

5. A borrower will pay an interest rate determined and influenced by all of the following except:

a. inflation expectations
b. the borrower's credit quality
c. the length of time over which the funds will be borrowed
d. bonds purchased by that borrower in the past

6. If a borrower pays 6.5% on a 2-year loan, and the expected rate of inflation is said to be 1.5%, what would be the real rate of interest on this loan?

a. 5%
b. 8%
c. 6.5%
d. 7%

7. All of the following are true of a company's balance sheet EXCEPT:

a. it communicates the value of a company in what it owns and what it owes
b. it acts as a great tool in telling an analyst whether a company is in an upward trend of improvement or a downward trend of decline
c. assets = liabilities + owner's equity
d. owner's equity is equal to a company's "net worth"

8. Which of the following are examples of assets found on a balance sheet?

I. prepaid expenses
II. accounts receivable
III. notes payable
IV. accrued taxes

a. II. only
b. III. and IV.
c. I. and II.
d. I. and IV.

9. Given the following balance sheet totals, calculate this company's working capital.

Total current assets:	$42,000,000
Total fixed assets:	$57,000,000
Total other assets:	$3,500,000
Total current liabilities:	$7,000,000
Total long-term liabilities:	$55,000,000

a. $35,000,000
b. $9,500,000
c. $40,500,000
d. $95,500,000

10. Calculate the dividend payout ratio, given the following income statement totals for company FNN.

Net income:	$5,750,000
Earnings per share:	$7.67
(given 750,000 common shares outstanding)	
Annual cash dividends:	$1,500,000

a. 3.8%
b. 26%
c. 133%
d. 38%

11. All of the following are true of a stock's pricing patterns and trendlines EXCEPT:

a. a head and shoulders bottom indicates that the future trend of the stock price will be downward
b. during a period of rising prices the trendline will connect all of the bottoms of the stock's price pattern
c. the validity of a stock's trendline depends on the number of times the price pattern touches it
d. the more times the price pattern touches the trendline, the more valid it is

12. Calculate the present value of $53,500 with receipt of these funds being taken 3 years (t) from today. The desired rate of return (r) for these funds is 9%.

a. $41,003.30
b. $41,311.82
c. $49,082.57
d. $42, 010.50

13. Which of the following measures of central tendency is defined as measuring the most common value in a given distribution of numbers?

a. mean
b. range
c. mode
d. median

14. Given the following 5-year annual returns for companies TRX, PFF, GRW, and SKT, which of the four would be a LEAST appropriate investment choice for a highly conservative investor?

	2010	2011	2012	2013	2014
TRX.	-1%.	4%.	2%.	7%.	4.50%
PFF.	1%.	6%.	-1.5%.	8%.	11%
GRW.	6%.	-4%.	18%.	12%.	1%
SKT.	7%.	9.5%.	10.75%.	11%.	8%

a. company SKT
b. company GRW
c. company TRX
d. company PFF

15. All of the following are examples of systematic risk EXCEPT:

a. financial risk
b. interest rate risk
c. purchasing power risk
d. market risk

16. Which of the following types of risk can be minimized simply through the diversification of a portfolio?

a. market risk
b. systematic risk
c. business risk
d. purchasing power risk

17. If the Federal Reserve were to suddenly increase interest rates, all of the following would be a possible result EXCEPT:

a. valuation models may be adjusted to account for the impending rate change impact
b. stock market may decline
c. certain highly leveraged companies may feel a negative effect
d. bond prices would also increase

18. Which of the following bond strategies involves multiple bond purchases, made at potentially different times, and with all maturing at one single time?

a. bullets
b. ladders
c. barbells
d. none of the above

19. An investor would like to reduce his liquidity risk. Which of the following would best be a strategy he could utilize to do that?

a. invest in mutual funds
b. diversify his investments across cash, fixed income investments, equities, and hard assets
c. maintain a portion of his assets in cash and cash equivalent asserts
d. invest in fixed income diversifying across different maturity dates

20. Which of the following are TRUE of money market instruments?

I. the borrower is the buyer of the instrument
II. long-term loanable funds bought and sold as securities in the money market
III. buying and selling these instruments involves the trading of money not cash
IV. the money lender is the seller of the instrument

a. III. only
b. I. and IV.
c. I., II., III., and IV.
d. II. and III.

21. Certificates of deposit (CD's):

a. must have a face value of at least $10,000
b. are secured time deposits
c. pay periodic interest
d. have guaranteed rates of return

22. All of the following are true of Treasury securities EXCEPT:

a. no credit risk
b. trades with narrow spreads
c. high liquidity in secondary markets
d. interest is subject to state income tax

23. TIPS:

I. provides an investor with an interest payment that will decrease during inflationary times
II. are issued with 5-, 10-, and 30-year maturities
III. primarily provide an investor with protection from "financial risk"
IV. pay interest to an investor every 6 months

a. I., II., and III.
b. II. and IV.
c. I. and IV.
d. II., III., and IV.

24. When considering most other securities, which of the following is a unique characteristic of Ginnie Mae?

a. payments to investors consist of only interest
b. investor receives annual payments
c. payments to investors are the result of fees associated with home mortgages
d. pools of home mortgages underlie the security

25. Company TWR's stock is currently trading at $55.50 per share. How many shares of TWR would a bond investor receive at conversion if the conversion price is $75?

a. 133 shares
b. 1 share
c. 13 shares
d. 18 shares

26. Which of the following are examples of the income sources utilized to provide payments to municipal bondholders?

I. the sale of a property that is delinquent on the payment of taxes
II. toll bridge earnings
III. property taxes
IV. lease rentals

a. I., II., III., and IV.
b. III. only
c. I., II., and III.
d. II. and III.

27. Place the following in order of corporate liquidation priority.

I. subordinated debt
II. preferred stockholders
III. mortgage bonds
IV. debentures

a. III., I., IV., II.
b. IV., III., II., I.
c. IV., I., III., II.
d. III., IV., I., II.

28. Investment-grade bonds are rated by Standard & Poor's as which of the following or higher?

a. BB
b. A
c. BBB
d. AA

29. All of the following are true of an investor purchasing a bond at a premium to par EXCEPT:

a. the bond was sold to the investor at a price above par
b. par value is greater than what the investor paid for the bond
c. the yield is lower than the coupon rate
d. if held to maturity, the investor will receive back par value

30. An investor purchases a bond paying $925 for it. If annual interest is fixed at 11.5%, what can this investor expect to GAIN (over his initial investment) in total from this investment if held to maturity (here, 5 years)?

a. $650
b. $575
c. $115
d. $75

31. All of the following are benefits to owning common stock EXCEPT:

a. can act as an excellent hedge against inflation
b. right to vote for company directors
c. in the event of a company bankruptcy, has a priority claim over preferred shareholders
d. risk is limited only to investment made

32. Preferred stock is often viewed as a fixed income investment for which of the following reasons?

a. fixed rate of return
b. scheduled redemption date
c. preset maturity date
d. guaranteed monthly dividends

33. Which of the following types of preferred stock has its value linked to that of common stock?

a. cumulative
b. convertible
c. callable
d. adjustable-rate

34. Characteristic(s) of emerging market investments include:

I. low commission rates
II. lack of transparency
III. potential for rapid growth rate
IV. liquidity issues

a. I., II., III., and IV.
b. I., II., and IV.
c. IV. only
d. II., III., and IV.

35. An employee exercises an incentive stock option to purchase shares of his company's stock and after some period of time has proceeded with the sale of those shares. Under which of the following conditions would any profits made on that sale NOT be reported as long-term capital gains?

a. held stock for one and half years after date of exercise, sold two and half years after grant
b. held stock for eleven months after date of exercise, sold two years after grant
c. held stock for one year after date of exercise, sold two years after grant
d. held stock for four years after date of exercise, sold three years after grant

36. The category of defensive industry stocks include all of the following types of consumer goods companies EXCEPT:

a. energy
b. food
c. pharmaceuticals
d. automobiles

37. Which of the following is NOT among the most useful economic indicators?

a. a measure of inflation
b. a measure of volatility/risk
c. a measure of a nation's total output
d. a measure of imports vs exports

38. Closed-end investment companies:

I. may offer common stock, bonds, and preferred stock
II. are publicly traded funds
III. will have as their initially offering an open offering, registered as such with the SEC
IV. have their bid and ask price determined by supply and demand

a. I., II., and IV.
b. II. and III.
c. I. and III.
d. II. and IV.

39. Given the following information, calculate the net asset value (NAV) per share of the mutual fund GROWTH.

fund common stock asset value: $235,500
fund bond asset value: $65,750
fund liabilities value: $36,000
shares outstanding: 2,500

a. $94.20
b. $120.50
c. $79.80
d. $106.10

40. Nonfixed unit investment trusts (UITs):

a. are actively involved in managing their own portfolios
b. employ an investment advisor
c. buy shares of an underlying mutual fund
d. have their own board of directors

41. All of the following are reasons to invest in real estate investment trusts (REITs) EXCEPT:

a. provide investors with dividends and investment gains without passing losses onto them
b. provide for dividends to avoid being taxed at the full ordinary income rate
c. provide for an investment in real estate without the degree of liquidity risk experienced with actual real estate ownership
d. allow for higher degree of portfolio diversification

42. Exchange traded funds (ETFs):

I. are not considered a "pooled investment vehicle"
II. can be purchased on margin
III. associated with public indexes of only stocks and bonds
IV. expenses are lower than a mutual fund with more minimal fees

a. II. and IV.
b. I. only
c. I. and III.
d. II., III., and IV.

43. Which combination below would be considered a premium bond given only the coupon and current yield information?

a. coupon: 6, current yield: 7%
b. coupon: 7%, current yield: 7%
c. coupon: 7%, current yield: 7.25%
d. coupon: 7.5%, current yield: 6%

44. All of the following would be considered an "in-the-money" option EXCEPT:

a. MGA 34 call when MGA stock's current price is at $36
b. HNY 43 call when HNY stock's current price is at $41
c. PPL 65 call when PPL stock's current price is at $75
d. RST 35 put when RST stock's current price is at $31

45. Which of the following describes a reason an investor should invest in a hedge fund?

a. investment participation of fund management
b. ease of liquidity
c. minimal expenses
d. lower relative risk for large loss of capital

46. Limited partnerships have at least one general and one limited partner. Which of the following describes responsibilities assumed by a general partner within the partnership?

a. buys but cannot sell property
b. maintains at least a 10% financial interest
c. supervises limited aspects of the business
d. bears direct and joint liability

47. The following are all characteristics of a variable annuity EXCEPT:

a. salesmen require licenses for both securities and insurance
b. keeps pace with inflation
c. investor contributions are placed and kept in the insurance company's general account
d. involve an investment in a portfolio of money market instruments, debt, and equities

48. With regards to index annuities, there are different ways that interest due to growth will be credited to an account. Which of the following methods involves comparing the calculated interest on the index value at the beginning and end of the contract?

a. high-water mark
b. point-to-point
c. annual reset
d. low-water mark

49. Which of the following are TRUE of the accumulation stage of an annuity?

I. is considered the pay-in stage
II. provides for flexibility in contract terms
III. termination of the contract is restricted during this time
IV. missed periodic payments will not result in forfeiting prior contributions

a. I., II., and IV.
b. I. and IV.
c. III. and IV.
d. II. only

50. An investor would like to choose an annuity payout option that will provide for payments to continue after his death until the entire initial principal has been provided for. Which of the following payout options should this investor choose given those specifications?

a. life annuity with period certain
b. straight life
c. refund annuity
d. mortality guarantee

51. Which of the following describes a person who is a director, officer, partner, or employee of an investment adviser but whose function does NOT require registration as defined under the Investment Advisers Act of 1940?

a. broker
b. associated person
c. dealer
d. supervised person

52. Under the SEC Release 1A-1092, all of the following can be considered an investment adviser except:

a. persons who provide advice or analyses
b. persons who are compensated, either directly or indirectly, for providing analyses or advice
c. persons who provide securities related investment advice, reports, or analyses
d. persons who do business providing advice or analyses

53. Which of the following individuals could be considered an investment adviser under the Investment Advisers Act of 1940?

I. a sports agent
II. a pension consultant
III. a financial planner
IV. an entertainer's manager

a. II. and III.
b. III. and IV.
c. I., II., III., and IV.
d. I., II., and III.

54. An investment adviser who does not have a place of business in the state of Arizona and is registered in the state of California, would NOT be considered exempt from registration within the state of Arizona given which of the following circumstances?

a. his only clients within the state of Arizona total 6, and they've all been residents of the state during the previous 12 months
b. his only clients are not actually residents of the state of Arizona, but instead are only temporarily in the state
c. his only clients are also investment advisers
d. his only clients are institutional investors who have assets of more than $1,000,000

55. All of the following meet the definition of what an investment adviser representative is EXCEPT:

a. acts as a team of two individuals working as representatives of an investment advisory firm
b. manages accounts
c. provides advice regarding securities
d. makes decisions regarding the securities advice to be provided

56. Which of the following qualify as an investment adviser representative's (IAR's) "place of business" and accordingly, provide for the requirement that he register in that state as stipulated in the Investment Advisers Act of 1940?

I. IAR has an office that he travels to twice a month to have lunch with a fellow friend who works in that office
II. IAR participates weekly in a basketball league with fellow representatives from the local investment office
III. IAR has an office to which he travels twice a month to meet with clients in the local area
IV. IAR publicizes monthly that he will be providing his investment advisory services to local clients at a YMCA hall

a. I. and IV.
b. I. and III.
c. III. and IV.
d. I., II., and III.

57. Investment adviser representatives (IAR):

a. must not provide only impersonal investment advice in order to stay qualified as an IAR
b. are not at risk of registration revocation simply due to the occurrence of bankruptcy
c. must register with the state as well as the SEC
d. require meeting a net worth threshold in order to register

58. Regarding the termination of an investment adviser representative (IAR), all of the following are true EXCEPT:

a. if the adviser involved is covered federally, the IAR must notify the administrator
b. similar to the termination of an agent, a Form U-5 must be filed
c. if registered through the state, notification must be given to the administrator by the IAR's firm
d. similar to the termination of an agent, all involved parties are obligated to notify the administrator

59. A principal is all of the following except:

a. a bond's face value
b. the role a dealer takes on within a transaction
c. a firm employee who participates in a supervisory role
d. the monthly payments made to an investor

60. The role of a dealer includes which of the following?

I. acts as a principal in transactions
II. charges a commission
III. is not a market maker
IV. takes on risk during transactions

a. I. only
b. I. and IV.
c. I., II., and IV.
d. II. and III.

61. A broker:

a. takes on his or her own risk in transactions
b. charges either a markup or markdown
c. participates in orders on his or her client's behalf, acting as an agent
d. acts as a market maker

62. Which of the following are considered exclusions to the broker/dealer definition?

I. investment firms
II. issuers
III. agents
IV. banks

a. II. and III.
b. I., II., and III.
c. II., III., and IV.
d. II. only

63. Which of the following satisfies the definition of "agent"?

a. corporation
b. individual
c. brokerage firm
d. legal person

64. Which of the following are TRUE regarding a broker/dealer's ministerial employees:

a. because they are classified as clerical and administrative, they are always exempt from the registration requirement regardless of the extent to which they may or may not participate in efforts that are securities related
b. they are excluded from receiving any year-end annual bonuses, even those based on the company's overall profits and performance
c. they are customarily excluded from the definition of "agent", and accordingly, need not be registered as a requirement for their employment
d. providing a quote as requested by a client would qualify as acting as an "agent" and accordingly, would require their registration as a requirement for performing their job

65. Which of the following describes an activity that would NOT require the employee to be registered as an agent?

a. an employee prequalifies clients for specific firm services
b. an employee makes recommendations over the phone to clients regarding increasing profits within their stock portfolio
c. a summer intern is paid for each client with whom she makes contact regarding potential activity in his portfolio
d. an employee asks a client over the phone if he would like to receive general information regarding the firm's services

66. Which of the following transactions describes an instance when the employee of an issuer is considered to be an "agent"?

a. those with financial institutions
b. private placements
c. those between an issuer and underwriter
d. if the employee received commissions

67. Per the Uniform Securities Act, which of the following are considered "securities" and are, therefore, held to the provisions of the act?

I. fixed annuity contract
II. commodities
III. debentures
IV. collateral trust certificates

a. I., II., and III.
b. III. and IV.
c. II. and IV.
d. I., III., and IV.

68. All of the following are allowable when considering the Uniform Securities Act EXCEPT:

a. sale of an unregistered nonexempt security
b. sale of an unregistered exempt security
c. unregistered sale of currencies
d. sale of registered nonexempt security

69. What is another term used to describe a "secondary transaction"?

a. exempt transaction
b. issuer transaction
c. non-issuer transaction
d. dependent transaction

70. An investor makes the request to his broker that he would only like to participate in issuer transactions. Which of the following would be appropriate for this investor?

I. an initial public offering
II. a subsequent public offering
III. a primary offering
IV. secondary transactions

a. I. only
b. I., II., and III.
c. I. and III.
d. I., III., and IV.

71. An order is entered by the Administrator that suspends the registration of a securities professional. Which of the following is not required for that order to become final?

a. there must be an effort to seek out the facts of the circumstance, provide written documentation to support those findings, and then formulate conclusions that are based in law
b. an opportunity for a hearing must be provided
c. all the necessary notices to all of the involved parties must be given
d. criminal charges brought against the offending securities professional

72. A state Administrator in California would normally require which of the following on an issuer application?

I. notice of any adverse judgment by the SEC associated with the offering
II. the amount of securities to be offered in the state of California
III. any additional states in which the securities will be offered
IV. the amounts of securities to be offered in any additional states

a. I., II., and III.
b. II. only
c. II., III., and IV.
d. I., II., III., and IV.

73. All of the following are true regarding broker/dealer capital requirements EXCEPT:

a. may be set by the broker/dealer's state Administrator
b. a broker/dealer who has met the net capital requirement set for him by the SEC may still need to satisfy the capital requirement set by his state Administrator, if higher
c. considered to be a broker/dealer's liquidated net worth
d. if met by the broker/dealer, no posting of bond will be required

74. Of the powers that are retained by an Administrator, which of the following are associated with BOTH the registration of individuals and securities?

a. summary order
b. stop order
c. cease and desist order
d. limit order

75. An adviser has had two material legal actions against her. The first occurred at the beginning of her career, 14 years ago, and the second occurred 8 years ago. Which of the following are TRUE regarding these disclosures in relation to clients?

I. if the adviser is federally-covered, she has up to 48 hours before entering into the contract with the client to personally disclose these legal actions
II. if the adviser is state-covered, the disclosures regarding these legal actions should be made to prospective clients regardless of when they occurred
III. if the legal actions occurred within the last 10 years, a state-covered adviser has until the point of actually entering into a contract with her client, given that client has the right to terminate that contract without penalty
IV. for federally-covered advisers, disclosures of this nature are made via a brochure provided to the client

a. II. only
b. III. and IV.
c. I. and II.
d. IV. only

76. In an effort to protect investors of new issues, the Securities Act of 1933 does all of the following except:

a. provide added protections for those committing fraud in the issuance of an offering of new securities
b. requires the issuer of an offering to provide accurate disclosures regarding the offering
c. requires that an investor have made available to him all material information regarding the offering he may require in determining its merits and impacting his decision to invest
d. requires the issuer of an offering to provide accurate disclosures regarding itself

77. A passive management style is characterized by:

a. achieving higher returns by trading in and out of stocks
b. utilizing market timing to outperform a market index
c. putting together a portfolio of securities that will mimic the activity and performance of a market index
d. focusing on fewer market sectors to achieve higher returns

78. Opportunity cost is:

a. reduced by diversification
b. avoidable
c. the risk that an investor will not be able to liquidate their investment at a time of their choosing
d. the return given up on other investments when you choose a specific investment

79. Of the following individuals, which would NOT be considered an investment adviser and subject to regulation?

a. an individual who has just graduated with an MBA in finance publishes an online newsletter offering general comments on where she sees the future direction of the overall market going
b. a financial analyst who is employed by a firm to create general sector market reports meets with a client to offer advice on specific securities within those sectors
c. an entertainment representative receives a percentage compensation from the salaries paid to his client for acting, but also occasionally advises the client on securities in which she should be investing
d. an individual acting as a broker/dealer representative makes recommendations to a client regarding specific securities

80. Which of the following is NOT true regarding adviser compensation?

a. advisory fees may be paid by a third party and need not be paid directly by the recipient of the advice
b. "special compensation" for advisory services go beyond the fees paid for typical broker/dealer services
c. advisory services must be charged separately from other broker/dealer services
d. compensation may include commissions

81. Section 28(e)'s safe harbor provision of the Securities Exchange Act of 1934 detail all of the following EXCEPT:

a. research provided must be proprietary in nature
b. brokerage services can include transaction settlement
c. research can be provided via publications
d. research services can include portfolio analysis and strategy

82. The following include some examples of "soft dollar compensation". Which would NOT be covered under 28(e) of the Securities Exchange Act of 1934?

a. an investment adviser receives analytical software
b. an investment adviser receives payment to cover travel expenses incurred while attending a research seminar
c. an investment adviser is provided an invitation and then attends a research conference put on by the broker/dealer firm
d. an investment adviser receives research reports analyzing the current and future performance of one specific company

83. With regard to the NASAA model rule, an adviser should provide which of the following safeguards related to the direct fee deduction arrangement he made with his clients' accounts?

a. notice of unique or one-time fees being deducted but not recurring fees being deducted
b. verbal authorization to be able to deduct advisory fees
c. provide notice of safeguards
d. make a verbal request before each fee is deducted

84. Discretionary trading authority is provided to:

I. a business manager to which you have executed a document granting authority to, even though the manager hasn't taken receipt of the actual written document yet
II. a business partner who has taken possession of a written document stating trading authorization has been granted to him
III. an attorney to which an individual has given his power of attorney
IV. an attorney to which an individual has given written authority to trade

a. II. and IV.
b. II. and III.
c. I., II., and IV.
d. I., II., III., and IV.

85. All of the following are true of a fiduciary EXCEPT:

a. may be acting as the receiver in a bankruptcy
b. may not assign any portion of the responsibilities to a third party, including assuming the role of portfolio management and security selection unless and until another fiduciary is named
c. may be acting as a trustee for a trust account
d. she is limited in the securities she may purchase if operating in a legal list state

86. Per ERISA provisions, a fiduciary must:

a. act as cautiously as the average person
b. maximize profits even while assuming larger risk if necessary
c. act as prudent as the average expert
d. maximize profits while minimizing risk

87. An individual opens an account for which she refuses to provide the information necessary to satisfy the suitability requirements needed to properly service the account. Which of the following are TRUE regarding this scenario?

I. if the account is with an investment adviser, it must be refused until the suitability information is provided by the individual
II. if the account is with an investment adviser, the account may be opened but only to transact unsolicited orders
III. if the account is with a broker/dealer, the account may be opened but only to transact unsolicited orders
IV. if the account is with a broker/dealer, the account may be opened with no restrictions on transacting both solicited and unsolicited orders

a. II. and III.
b. I. and IV.
c. I. and III.
d. I. only

88. Per the Uniform Securities Act, which of the following would be an allowable action to be performed by a security professional?

a. a security professional borrows cash from his client, Union Bank, repaying the loan in a timely manner
b. a client gives discretionary authority over her account to her security professional, that individual borrows cash from the client's account, and then quickly repays the loan
c. a security professional lends cash to a client that is also a longtime friend and business associate
d. a security professional lends cash to his client, Union Bank, from another financial institution client

89. A violation of insider trading:

a. occurs every time a person trades while in possession of that company's nonpublic information
b. can be punishable by the payment of treble damages
c. only requires intent to trade on the nonpublic information
d. can only be committed by company executives

90. Which of the following would NOT be considered a permissible practice?

a. a broker/dealer authorizes his agent in writing to execute a transaction that will then not be recorded on the regular books and records of the firm
b. establishing an account that is fictitious for the purpose of executing transactions that are prohibited in nature
c. with prior written authorization from the client and broker/dealer, an agent shares in the profits of their client's accounts
d. a security professional borrows cash from his client, Union Bank, repaying the loan in a timely manner

91. An account where one beneficial non-business owner has singular control over the investments in the account, as well as the ability to request distributions from the account is:

a. a joint tenants with right of survivorship
b. an individual account
c. sole proprietorship
d. a tenants in common

92. All of the following are true of a general partner EXCEPT:

a. decisions made will be binding to partnership
b. buys and sells property related to the partnership
c. is required to maintain a financial interest in the partnership of at least 3%
d. bears direct and joint liability

93. An individual considering becoming a limited partner in a limited partnership can expect his role to include:

I. acting as a passive investor
II. assuming responsibility for some limited operational functions of the partnership
III. taking no personal responsibility for any indebtedness that the partnership experiences
IV. taking receipt of the partnerships gains and cash distributions

a. I., III., and IV.
b. II. and IV.
c. I. only
d. III. only

94. Of the following business structures, which provides the owner with limited liability and a pass-through of both profits and losses?

I. C corporation
II. limited liability company (LLC)
III. limited partnership
IV. S corporation

a. II., III., and IV.
b. I. and II.
c. II. and III.
d. III. and IV.

95. Compiling a client's financial profile would involve assessing all of the following EXCEPT:

a. retirement account information
b. security holdings and their value
c. credit card debt totals
d. work history

96. A client's non-financial profile is just as crucial for an adviser to compile as his financial one. All of the following non-financial items would be relevant to request EXCEPT:

a. historical stability of the individual's employment
b. future educational needs for the individual or family
c. investment knowledge and experience
d. credit card debt totals

97. An investment adviser has just taken on a new client. In an effort to understand this client's risk tolerance, which of the following should she discuss with her client?

I. ability to tolerate a variety of market fluctuations
II. number of dependents and their ages
III. time horizon, long or short
IV. current employment status

a. I., III., and IV.
b. I. and III.
c. I., II., and III.
d. I. only

98. An individual's incidents of ownership in a life insurance policy can be evidenced by his ability to do all of the following except:

a. assign ownership of the policy
b. designate a beneficiary
c. borrow money from policy in excess of the cash value of the policy
d. modify the policy

99. Modern Portfolio Theory:

I. theoretically stands for the idea that risk can be diversified away by building a certain type of portfolio
II. promotes diversification as a risk reducer which will then cause an increase in returns
III. analyzes the specifics of individual stocks within the portfolio
IV. proves that a higher level of portfolio volatility will produce better returns

a. I., II., III., and IV.
b. I. and II.
c. III. and IV.
d. I. only

100. The efficient frontier is all of the following EXCEPT:

a. provides a reference point for evaluating portfolios, below which lie the inefficient, lower return/higher risk portfolios
b. plotted as a curve
c. used as a tool in constructing the most efficient portfolio
d. made up of portfolios generally providing the most return

101. Which version of the Efficient Market Hypothesis is based on the idea that current security pricing already reflects all public information that is available?

a. strong-form
b. weak-form
c. semi-strong form
d. complete form

102. Which of the following is true of valuation ratios?

a. they provide the information needed to purchase a security
b. they are a comparison of two specific numbers taken from the balance sheet
c. they compare share price to relevant company data to help analyze performance
d. they include the current ratio and quick ratio

103. An investment adviser has a client whose style involves giving great focus to the proportion of types of assets that make up, and essentially balance, his long-term portfolio. Which of the following investment styles should he target in seeking a money manager that would best suit his needs?

a. tactical asset allocation
b. strategic asset allocation
c. asset class allocation
d. market movement allocation

104. A client's portfolio was opened with an asset mix of 55% equity/45% debt. The total initial investment was $80,000. By the end of the first year, this portfolio climbed to a total asset value of $105,000, with equity portion growing to $69,000. If the client's objectives require keeping the portfolio balanced in its original 55% equity/45% debt proportions, what action will need to be taken to do that?

a. sell $11,000 in equities, buy $11,000 in debt
b. sell $22,000 in equities, buy $22,000 in debt
c. sell $22,000 in debt, buy $22,000 in equities
d. sell $11,000 in debt, buy $11,000 in equities

105. A client has a portfolio with a total asset value of $150,000. Under her "constant dollar" investment plan, she would like to optimally maintain $110,000 in stocks, with the other $40,000 then invested in debt. If the stocks in her portfolio were to increase to $135,000, what action would need to be taken in order to keep the portfolio at this client's optimal constant dollar goal?

a. invest an additional $7,250 in debt
b. buy $17,750 in additional stocks
c. take $25,000 in stock gains and reinvest in debt
d. buy $40,000 in additional stocks

106. An active portfolio management style:

I. requires a manager with consistently successful market timing abilities
II. seeks to construct a portfolio that will essentially mimic a market index
III. is similar to tactical asset allocation
IV. prefers low-cost strategies for generating returns

a. I. and III.
b. II. and IV.
c. II., III., and IV.
d. I. only

107. Which stock characteristic would be sought out by a growth style investment manager?

a. those that are priced low relative to the company's earnings
b. those with a low P/E ratio
c. those that are at a 52-week price high
d. those that show great future growth potential based solely on the information found in the company's financial statements

108. All of the following are true of portfolio diversification EXCEPT:

a. involves stocks being chosen because of their negative correlation to each other
b. reduces unsystematic risk
c. causes business risk to decrease as returns increase
d. it maximizes short-term gains

109. Dollar cost averaging:

I. involves investing varying amounts of money at varying times in an effort to seek out only pricing lows for that security
II. has the investor increasing the number of shares she purchases when prices are low, and decreasing the number purchased when prices are high
III. seeks to achieve purchasing a security over time at an average cost that is lower than its average price over the same period
IV. reduces the risk of purchasing shares at a high

a. I. and IV.
b. II., III., and IV.
c. III. only
d. II. and III.

110. Which of the following is TRUE of progressive taxes?

a. consume a larger percentage of income for those with lower incomes
b. one type is a payroll tax
c. these are more demanding of individuals with high incomes
d. it is the same as a flat tax

111. For the current year, an individual will be taxed at a rate of 27% for any amount earned that is greater than $155,000, and up to $310,000. At that level the rate jumps to 31% for any excess above that. Should the individual's income increase to greater than $435,500, the tax rate will also increase to 33%. If an individual were to report annual earnings of $301,750, what would be the individual's marginal tax rate?

a. 27%
b. 33%
c. 31%
d. 25%

112. An investor purchases 120 shares of SFT stock for $24 per share, and 210 shares of PLT stock for $21 per share. If this investor were to sell his 120 shares of SFT for $35 per share and all 210 shares of PLT for $22.50 per share, what would be this investor's total capital gain for tax purposes?

a. $2,055
b. $1,320
c. $315
d. $1,635

113. A 64-year-old man dies leaving a gross estate worth $12,755,000. His estate incurs funeral expenses totaling $32,551 and he leaves behind credit card debts totaling $4,887, and multiple mortgages totaling $1,660,233. Determine what this man's adjusted gross estate (AGE) would be.

a. $12,717,562
b. $11,057,329
c. $12,787,551
d. $11,062,216

114. A client would like to open a traditional individual retirement account (IRA). Which of the following would NOT qualify (per the IRS) as compensation for the purposes of his contributing to such an account?

a. self-employment income
b. alimony
c. pension income
d. tips

115. Roth individual retirement accounts (IRAs):

I. individuals have a maximum limit on contributions of $8,000 per year
II. withdrawal of contributions can be done tax-free
III. contributions are not tax-deductible
IV. distributions from the account must begin at 72 years old

a. I. and IV.
b. II., III., and IV.
c. I. only
d. II. and III.

116. An eligible employee is considering a variety of investment vehicles for his 403(b) plan. Which of the following would be allowable choices for him?

I. annuities
II. commercial paper
III. money market mutual fund
IV. life insurance policies

a. I. and III.
b. I. only
c. I., II., and III.
d. III. and IV.

117. Regarding the concept of "prudent investing", the Uniform Prudent Investor Act (UPIA) provided all of the following adjustments to the Employment Retirement Income Security Act of 1974 (ERISA) EXCEPT:

a. prudence standard is not simply applied to choices regarding individual investments, but instead to investments, as they are part of a total portfolio
b. additional restrictions were added regarding the types of investments that were allowable for trustees to invest in
c. a fiduciary's primary concern must be with balancing risk versus return
d. enabled greater diversification in investment portfolios

118. ERISA (Employment Retirement Income Security Act of 1974) guidelines include all of the following EXCEPT:

a. there must be a specified time by which employees are entitled to receive their retirement benefits
b. as long as a retirement plan is offered, anyone 21 years or older within the company must be covered
c. the plan must be provided in writing with annual updates also provided to the employees
d. employee benefits and contributions are determined impartially per a formula method

119. Per ERISA guidelines, the following are TRUE of fiduciaries:

I. they must seek to minimize plan and investment expenses
II. they must not proceed with investment decisions based on the amount of transaction costs involved
III. they must be held to the "prudent person" standard
IV. they must employ diversification in order to minimize large losses

a. I., II., and III.
b. III. and IV.
c. I., II., and IV.
d. I. only

120. Coverdell ESAs:

a. allow for multiple contributions to be made to one account but not in excess of $2,000 per child per year
b. require that earnings must not be tax-deferred
c. provide for contributions to be tax-deductible
d. provides for distributions to always be tax-free as long as used for educational expenses

121. According to the Uniform Securities Act, which of the following is true regarding advertisements for investment advisors?

a. advertisements may include unpaid testimonials
b. all advertising limitations are specific to medium (TV, print, email, social media, etc.)
c. when referencing performance of investment adviser recommendations, they must include those resulting in losses as well as those resulting in gains
d. they must include messages about the investment adviser directed to one individual

122. Which of the following are characteristics of a college savings plan?

I. no residency requirement
II. limited enrollment period
III. no age limits
IV. no state guarantee

a. I., III., and IV.
b. II. and IV.
c. I., II., III., and IV.
d. II. and III.

123. An individual would like to rollover the unused portion of his 529 plan to a member of his immediate family. Which of the following would NOT be considered immediate family?

a. his stepbrother's spouse
b. his foster child
c. his first cousin
d. his stepbrother's father

124. Which of the following types of orders is NOT guaranteed execution?

a. market order
b. stop order
c. limit order
d. stop loss order

125. Which of the following are associated with the OTC market?

I. regulated by the NYSE
II. security prices are established through negotiation
III. government and municipal bonds trade there
IV. trade listed securities

a. II. only
b. II. and III.
c. I., II., III., and IV.
d. IV. only

126. How would a quote be stated for stock PLS with a bid price of $21.00 and an ask price of $21.75?

a. 21.00/21.75
b. 21.00 and 21.75
c. 21 to .75
d. 21 + .75

127. Inflation adjusted returns are called:

a. net present value
b. real rates of return
c. expected return
d. internal rate of return

128. Calculate the TOTAL expected return for three investments with the following data:

security APL with a 37% probability of returning 9%
security CRT with a 24% probability of returning 17%
security FST with a 55% probability of returning 12%

a. 14.01%
b. 7.41%
c. 13%
d. 10.74%

129. An investor has a specific rate of return that he requires on an investment. Which of the following will best help him determine whether a certain investment will meet his required rate of return?

a. expected return
b. real return
c. internal rate of return
d. net present value

130. Answer premium, par, or discount where appropriate in completing each of the following statements:

Note: current yield (CY), yield to maturity (YTM), yield to call (YTC)
A bond with a YTM less than its YTC trades at ________.
A bond with a YTC greater than its CY trades at ________.
A bond with a YTM less than its CY trades at ________.

a. discount, premium, premium
b. premium, premium, discount
c. premium, discount, premium
d. discount, discount, premium

Answer Key and Explanations

1. D: All of the tools above are utilized by the FED (Federal Reserve Board) to influence the US economy, and specifically, the money supply EXCEPT the FED does NOT set the prime rate. That rate is determined by the larger commercial banks. Raising or reducing the discount rate does, however, impact member banks' ability to borrow funds from the FED; raising or reducing the reserve requirements for commercial banks dictates the amounts they must leave on deposit with the FED; and purchasing and selling US Treasury securities in the open market directly impacts the money supply by adding to the reserves of commercial banks from whom the purchases were made, and reducing bank reserves when securities are sold to them.

2. B: A business cycle pattern is impacted significantly by the increase or decrease of an economy's goods and services output, or Gross Domestic Product (GDP). Just prior to a trough in the business cycle, the economy is experiencing a contraction, NOT an expansion. An economic contraction known as a depression is characterized by a GDP decline lasting at least six consecutive quarters, NOT eight. An economic contraction known as a recession is characterized by a GDP decline lasting at least two consecutive quarters, NOT four.

3. A: Given that a business cycle trough is defined as the END portion of a declining pattern of economic business activity, it would accordingly be characterized by a positive forward outlook for consumer spending to increase, a gradual transition for the Gross Domestic Product (GDP) growth rate from a negative to a positive, and a moderate rate of inflation.

4. C: Inflation is characterized as a general economic price increase as measured by an index such as the consumer price index (CPI). Excessive demand is one contributing cause of inflation in that prices for goods will increase as the demand for those goods exceeds the current supply for those goods. As inflation increases, however, bond prices will DECREASE, and interest rates will INCREASE, and inflation inertia occurs when the inflation rate is seen to NOT be immediately impacted by changes in the economy.

5. D: A borrower will pay an interest rate determined and influenced by inflation expectations, the borrower's credit quality, and the length of time over which the funds will be borrowed.

6. A: real rate of interest = nominal rate of interest - expected rate of inflation

This borrower's nominal rate of interest is the actual rate being paid for the funds borrowed, which here is 6.5%. Therefore:

$$\text{real rate of interest} = 6.5\% - 1.5\% = 5\%$$

7. B: A company's balance sheet communicates the value of a company in what it owns and what it owes. The balance sheet equation states that a company's liabilities plus its owner's equity will equal its overall assets. Further, a company's owner's equity will indicate what its "net worth" is. The balance sheet, however, in only providing a snapshot of a company's value at one point in time, will NOT act as a great tool in telling an analyst whether a company is in an overall upward trend of improvement or a downward trend in decline.

8. C: Prepaid expenses are considered assets in that they involve items where a future entitled benefit is still yet to be realized. Accounts receivable are also assets, given that the company is entitled to receive them from customers as payment for goods and services it provided to them.

Notes payable and accrued taxes are NOT assets, but instead are considered to be current liabilities on the company's balance sheet.

9. A: Working capital represents the amount of cash a company has readily available to it at any given time and is utilized as a tool to measure liquidity (the degree to which a company can convert assets into cash).

$$\text{working capital} = \text{current assets} - \text{current liabilities}$$

$$\$42{,}000{,}000 - 7{,}000{,}000 = \$35{,}000{,}000$$

10. B:

$$\text{dividend payout ratio} = \frac{\text{annual dividends per common share}}{\text{earnings per share (EPS)}}$$

$$\text{dividends per share} = \frac{\text{annual cash dividends}}{\text{\# of common shares outstanding}}$$

$$\text{dividends per share} = \frac{\$1{,}500{,}000}{750{,}000} = \$2.00$$

$$\text{dividend payout ratio} = \frac{\$2.00}{\$7.67} = .26 = 26\%$$

11. A: A head and shoulders bottom indicates that the future trend of the stock price will be upward (NOT downward) given that the past pattern shows the stock price has already "bottomed out". During a period of rising prices, the trendline will connect all of the bottoms of the stock's price pattern, and the validity of a stock's trendline depends on the number of times the price pattern touches it with the higher the number indicating a higher level of validity.

12. B:

$$\text{present value (PV)} = \frac{\text{future value (FV)}}{(1+r)^t}$$

$$\text{PV} = \frac{\$53{,}500}{(1+.09)^3}$$

$$= \frac{\$53{,}500}{(1.09)^3}$$

$$= \frac{\$53{,}500}{1.295029}$$

$$= \$41{,}311.82$$

13. C: The measure of central tendency that is defined as measuring the most common value in a given distribution of numbers is the mode. The mean is also known as the average, and is calculated by taking the sum of all values and dividing by the number of values. The range is the calculated difference between the high and low values in a distribution, and the median is the value that appears at the midpoint in the distribution.

14. B: A conservative investor would be seeking in an investment choice one that would provide the LEAST amount of annual return volatility. The standard deviation of each company's annual returns provides information regarding the dispersion and variance of values from the mean (average) of all of the 5 return numbers for each company. The higher the standard deviation of the return values, the higher the return volatility.

	Low.	Mean.	High
TRX.	-1%.	3.3%.	7%
PFF.	-1.5%.	4.9%.	11%
GRW.	-4%.	6.6%.	18%
SKT.	7%.	9.25%.	11%

By observing the above information, company GRW would be the LEAST appropriate investment choice for this investor due to it having the HIGHEST amount of variance (high and low dispersion) from its mean return over the last 5 years.

15. A: Systematic risk is associated with the overall market and changes within it producing adverse effects for companies regardless of their specific current condition or performance. Examples of this type of risk are interest rate risk (the risk of interest rate fluctuations), purchasing power risk (the risk of inflation), and market risk (the risk of an overall market decline due to an event outside of individual companies and their performance). Financial risk is NOT a systematic risk and instead is an unsystematic risk in that it is the type of risk that will be unique to only a specific industry or company. It involves a company's debt financing and its ongoing ability to meet its financial obligations.

16. C: Business risk can be greatly minimized through the diversification of a portfolio in that it is a risk that is related to the operations of only one specific company. The overall return of the portfolio can be hedged by investing in other companies not experiencing the same operational issues. Market and purchasing power risk are both types of systematic risk which is a nondiversifiable type of risk and involves changes in the market that can negatively affect ALL companies and industries. This type of risk will NOT be minimized by diversifying a portfolio.

17. D: If the Federal Reserve were to suddenly increase interest rates, bond prices would decrease, NOT increase. Further, valuation models may need to be adjusted to account for the impending rate change impact, which could then trigger a decline in the stock market. It would also be likely that certain leveraged companies who are more susceptible to interest rate risk may feel a more negative effect than others.

18. A: A bullet is a bond strategy that involves making multiple bond purchases, at potentially different times, and with all maturing at one single time. The investor here is trying to exploit the changes in interest rates over time while collectively capturing all gains at one single time at maturity. A ladder strategy involves purchasing a group of bonds at the same time up front, and then, having them all maturing at different times in the future. A barbell strategy involves only buying bonds with 1-2 year maturities and 10 or more year maturities, and is designed to take advantage of both long-term rates and quicker maturities.

19. C: An investor looking to reduce his liquidity risk would want to focus on maintaining a portion of his assets in cash and cash equivalents in order to have the ease of accessing some portion of his investments quickly and without any price or return issues. Purchasing mutual funds would target minimizing business risk; diversifying across all four asset classes will minimize market risk; and investing in fixed income assets of different maturities would minimize an investor's interest rate risk.

20. A: The buying and selling of money market instruments involves the trading of money (loanable funds), NOT cash. The instruments bought and sold are short-term loanable funds, NOT long-term. The lender acts as the buyer of the instrument, and the borrower is the seller.

21. C: Certificates of deposit (CDs) are the only money market instrument that pays periodic interest, and it's usually semiannually. CDs do not have a required face value; it is up to each individual bank to set a minimum deposit. CDs are considered unsecured deposits, as they lack assets pledged as collateral.

22. D: Treasury securities are NOT subject to state income tax. They are, however, highly liquid in the secondary markets and as a result of trading more actively, trade with narrow spreads. They also have no credit risk.

23. B: Treasury Inflation Protection Securities (TIPS) are issued with 5-, 10-, and 30-year maturities, and pay interest to an investor every 6 months. Further, they provide an investor with an interest payment that will increase, NOT decrease, during inflationary times and with that, provide the investor with protection from purchasing power (inflationary) risk, NOT financial risk which is associated with the risk of meeting debt obligations.

24. D: When considering most other securities, Ginnie Mae's are unique in that they pay monthly payments to investors, and those payments consist of both interest and principal. Also, pools of home mortgages underlie the security and are the source of the monthly investor payments. These payments are the homeowner's mortgage payments as they are then "passed through" to the investor.

25. C: The convertible bond represents a debt by company TWR of $1,000 and accordingly, in calculating the number of shares at conversion that par value is used along with the conversion price.

$$\frac{\$1{,}000}{\$75} = 13.33 = 13 \text{ shares}$$

The current price per share has no impact on the number of shares received at conversion in that the bond conversion is fixed at the time of the bond issuance.

26. A: There are two types of municipal bonds, general obligation bonds (GOs) and revenue bonds. General obligation bonds (GOs) pass along income received from sources such as property taxes or the sale of a delinquent property in order to satisfy obligations to bondholders. Revenue bonds may use toll bridge earnings or lease rental income to satisfy their obligations to bondholders.

27. D: In the event of corporate liquidation, the order of priority for paying off debt obligations is first, mortgage bonds as they are a secured debt security, second, debentures which are considered unsecured, third, subordinated debt which is junior to any other creditor, and last, preferred stockholders which are senior to common stockholders.

28. C: Institutions such as banks and insurance companies are generally only able to purchase bonds that are rated investment-grade or higher. For Standard & Poor's investment-grade level refers to a rating of BBB or higher, or specifically, the top four categories of bond ratings.

29. B: An investor purchasing a bond at a premium to par will be holding a bond that was sold to her at a price above par, and one where the yield is lower than the coupon rate. If held to maturity, this investor will receive back par value but that will be LESS than what she originally paid, NOT more.

30. A: If held to maturity, this investor first will receive back the par value of $1,000.

$$\$1{,}000 - \$925 = \$75$$

This will provide this investor with a GAIN of $75 above the discount to par value originally paid at the time of purchase.

Annual interest will be calculated as:

$$\$1{,}000 \times .115 = \$115$$

$$\$115 \times 5 \text{ years} = \$575$$

Total gain on investment:

$$\text{total annual interest over 5 years} + \text{gain from purchase at discount}$$

$$\$575 + \$75 = \$650$$

31. C: Benefits to owning common stock include providing the investor the right to vote for company directors, limiting risk only to the actual investment made, and utilizing the investment as a hedge against inflation in that historically returns tend to outpace the inflation rate. In the event of a company bankruptcy however, common shareholders do NOT have a priority claim above preferred shareholders in either asset liquidation or dividend payment.

32. A: Preferred stock is often viewed as a fixed income investment because of its fixed rate of return provided through a fixed dividend paid out quarterly. Preferred stock does NOT have a scheduled redemption date or a preset maturity date. It is in fact considered a perpetual security.

33. B: Convertible preferred stock has its value linked to the common stock shares that it can be converted into. The price for convertible preferred shares often moves in line with that of the common share price. Cumulative preferred stock accrues dividend payments, callable preferred stock can be bought back from investors by the issuing company, and adjustable-rate preferred stock is largely tied to interest rate movements, not the movement of the associated common stock.

34. D: Emerging market investments have high potential for rapid growth rates but tend to have higher potential for liquidity issues, and due to lower regulatory standards, have issues with a lack of transparency. Low commission rates are a characteristic of developed markets.

35. B: An employee exercising an incentive stock option to purchase shares of his company's stock, who then proceeds to sell those shares, will have any profit from said sale reported as ordinary income rather than long-term gains if the stock is held for eleven months after the exercise date, and the sale is made at least two years after grant. Profits in this scenario will be reported as long-term capital gains only if the stock is held for at least one year after date of exercise and sold at least two years after grant. Here, that is not the case.

36. D: Defensive industry stocks are largely companies that produce goods that are considered nondurable. Public consumption and demand for these types of goods will usually remain somewhat consistent and more predictable. Accordingly, these stocks will be less affected by the ups and downs of the normal business cycle. Energy, food, and pharmaceuticals are all considered defensive. Automobiles, however, are considered cyclical in that they are a durable good and demand for this type of good is much more sensitive to inflationary movements and fluctuations in the business cycle.

37. B: The five most commonly used economic indicators include 1. Gross Domestic Product – a measure of a nation's total output; 2. Employment indicators like the national unemployment rate; 3. Trade Deficit/Surplus – imports exceeding exports or vice versa; 4. Balance of payments – records of dealings between a country and all other countries over a period of time; and 5. Consumer Price index – a measure of inflation. Beta, a measure of volatility, is used to judge the relative risk of a given security or investment portfolio.

38. A: Closed-end investment companies may offer common stock, bonds, and preferred stock. They are publicly traded funds and have their bid and ask price determined by supply and demand. Their initial offering, however, would NOT be through an open offering but instead by registering a fixed amount of shares with the SEC and offering them to the public for a specific and limited period of time.

39. D:

$$\text{net asset value (NAV) per share} = \frac{\text{fund's total assets} - \text{liabilities}}{\text{\# of shares outstanding}}$$

$$\frac{(\$235{,}500 + \$65{,}750) - \$36{,}000}{2{,}500} = \frac{\$301{,}250 - \$36{,}000}{2{,}500} = \frac{\$265{,}250}{2{,}500} = \$106.10$$

40. C: Nonfixed unit investment trusts (UITs) buy shares of an underlying mutual fund. They do NOT, however, actively manage their own portfolios, employ an investment advisor, or have their own board of directors.

41. B: Benefits to investing in real estate investment trusts (REITs) include that they provide investors with dividends and investment gains without passing losses onto them, and provide for an investment in real estate without the degree of liquidity risk experienced with actual real estate ownership. REITs rarely perform exactly like other stocks or bonds, so they allow for a higher degree of portfolio diversification. However, they do not qualify for a reduced tax rate, and instead, dividends ARE taxed at full ordinary income rates.

42. A: Exchange traded funds (ETFs) can be purchased on margin, and have expenses that are generally lower than mutual funds including incurring more minimal fees. They are, however, considered a "pooled investment vehicle" and are associated with the public index of any class of asset, NOT just stocks and bonds.

43. D: When prices go down, yields will rise. A bond is considered to be trading at a premium when its current yield is less than its coupon. Additionally, a bond is considered to be trading at a discount when its current yoked is more than its coupon. Here, the premium bond is the one with a coupon at 7.5% and a current yield of 6% due to the current yield being less than the coupon.

44. B: An option that is in-the-money has intrinsic value in the amount that is equal to the difference between the option's strike price and the stock's price. A call option is in-the-money when the strike price is BELOW the stock's price. Here, the investor can exercise his or her option to purchase the stock at the lower price and immediately sell into the market at the higher current price of the stock. A put option is in-the-money when the strike price is ABOVE the stock's price. Here, the investor can exercise his or her option to sell the stock at the higher price and after having just purchased the stock in the market at the lower current price of the stock. Given the above explanation, here the HNY 43 call would NOT be considered in-the-money in that the stock's current price of $41 is less than the call's strike price of $43. This investor would not exercise an option to purchase stock at a price higher than what he or she could currently get in the market. The two other calls and one put would all be considered in-the-money.

45. A: One reason an investor should invest in a hedge fund is the fund management investing along with the other fund investors. When organized as a limited partnership, fund management will have its own money invested, tying it closer to the potential success or failure of the fund and accordingly, motivating it more to having it, in fact, succeed. Hedge funds, however, do have liquidity risk due to a lock-up period during which they may not make a withdrawal from the fund and their funds are not accessible. Further, expenses can be high, and due to the design of the fund involving relatively riskier strategies, the potential for larger loss of capital is very real.

46. D: Within a limited partnership, a general partner's responsibilities can include buying and selling property on behalf of the partnership, maintaining at least a 1% financial interest in the partnership, supervising all aspects of the partnership's business, and bearing direct and joint liability.

47. C: Variable annuities involve an investment in a portfolio of money market instruments, debt, and equities, which provide for an increased chance of keeping pace with inflation. Further, anyone participating in the sale of variable annuities must first obtain licenses for both securities and insurance. However, investor contributions that are made into variable annuities are placed and kept in a separate account from the insurance's company's general account, NOT the general account itself.

48. B: The point-to-point method involves comparing the calculated interest on the index value at the beginning of the contract to the value at the end of the contract. The high-water math method involves comparing the highest index value between anniversary dates to the value of the index at the beginning of the year. The annual reset method involves comparing simply the index value at the end of the year to the value at the beginning of the year.

49. A: An annuity's accumulation stage is considered the pay-in stage, provides for flexibility in contract terms, and the benefit of there being no risk of forfeiture of prior contributions should a payment be missed during this time. It is NOT true, however, that the holder of the contract cannot terminate his contract during this time, and in fact, he may terminate his contract at any time during this period.

50. C: This investor is seeking an annuity payout option that will provide for payments to continue after death until the entire initial principal has been provided for. The refund annuity option would meet those specifications, and would further provide for that payment refund to be in the form of a lump sum of cash or monthly payments. The life annuity with period certain option provides for the receipt of payments for life, but further guarantees a minimum period of time OR for life, whichever is longer. The straight life option simply provides for payments over the investor's life. The mortality guarantee involves the idea that payments are guaranteed for life regardless of whether the annuitant's life expectancy is increased or not.

51. D: Under the definitions of the Investment Advisers Act of 1940, a supervised person is a director, officer, partner, or employee of an investment adviser whose function does NOT require registration. The primary difference between associated persons and supervised persons involves the registration requirement. Associated persons are individuals who may be working in similar capacities, but ARE required to be registered.

52. A: Under the SEC Release 1A-1092, investment advisers are defined as those who participate in the business of providing advice or analyses, who provide securities related investment advice, reports, or analyses, and who are compensated, either directly or indirectly, for any of these services. Further, such a person will be required to become registered accordingly.

53. C: Under the Investment Advisers Act of 1940, an individual who offers advice, provides recommendations and further, is paid for those services, is in fact defined as an investment adviser and subject to the regulations of the Act. Both pension consultants and financial planners during the normal course of their everyday business would qualify as falling under the definition. Given the appropriate circumstances, both the sports agent and entertainer's manager may also fall under the definition of an investment adviser if they were to provide advice, or counsel regarding financial investments to someone they were under contract to represent.

54. A: This investment adviser would be exempt from registering with the state of Arizona if his only clients were not actually residents of the state of Arizona, but instead were only temporarily in the state, his only clients were also investment advisers, or his only clients were institutional investors who had assets of more than $1,000,000. He would NOT, however, be exempt from state registration in Arizona if his only clients within the state of Arizona totaled 6. The exemption applies only if the adviser has 5 or less clients within the state.

55. A: An investment adviser representative (IAR) may manage accounts, make decisions regarding the securities advice to be provided, and then actually provide securities advice. An IAR may NOT be a team of two or more, and must be an individual. This individual may represent an investment advisory firm.

56. C: "Place of business" as defined and stipulated in the Investment Advisers Act of 1940 provides for an office where the investment adviser representative (IAR) REGULARLY meets with clients and provides his services, or any other location that is represented to the general public as a place where the IAR communicates with clients and provides advisory services. Here, the locations that satisfy the definition of "place of business" are the office the IAR travels to twice a month to meet with local clients, and the YMCA hall where the IAR publicizes his services being offered to clients on a monthly basis. Both of these examples provide for the IAR providing his advisory services on a REGULAR basis, or a location that is represented to the public as a place where the IAR's advisory services will be provided. The office traveled to for lunch and the basketball league with fellow representatives from a local office do NOT qualify as "places of business" under the Act's definition.

57. A: Investment adviser representatives (IARs) must not provide only impersonal investment advice in order to stay qualified as an IAR, meaning any advice that is not meant to meet the financial objectives of SPECIFIC accounts. IARs must, however, ONLY register with the state, not the SEC, do NOT require meeting a net worth threshold in order to register, and do risk registration revocation simply due to the occurrence of bankruptcy.

58. D: Regarding the termination of an investment adviser representative (IAR), if the adviser involved is covered federally, the IAR must notify the administrator; if registered through the state, notification must be given to the administrator by the IAR's firm, and similar to the termination of an agent, a Form U-5 must be filed. UNLIKE the termination of an agent, all parties involved with the IAR's termination are NOT obligated to notify the administrator.

59. D: The term "principal" can take on different meanings within the securities industry. Its usage may be referring to a bond's face value, the role a dealer takes on within a transaction, or a firm employee who participates in a supervisory role.

60. B: Dealers act as principals in their own transactions, and accordingly take on their own risk during those transactions. They do NOT, however, charge commissions, and they DO in fact make markets in securities.

61. C: A broker's role includes participating in orders on his client's behalf and acting as an agent. He does NOT, however, charge a markup or markdown, act as market maker, or take on his own risk in transactions.

62. C: For regulatory purposes, issuers and agents are both considered to be exclusions to the broker/dealer definition. Banks are also excluded from the definition; however, the broker/dealer subsidiaries through which they transact in securities are NOT excluded. Investment firms, by transacting in the purchase and sale of securities as a business, are definitely NOT considered to be exclusions from the definition and accordingly, must register and are subject to securities regulation.

63. B: The term "agent" is defined as being ONLY an individual, or a natural person. Legal entities such as corporations and brokerage firms do NOT qualify as being an individual or natural person. They are instead considered to be a "legal person", and as such, are represented by an agent, for the purposes of participating in securities transactions.

64. C: A broker/dealer's ministerial employees are customarily excluded from the definition of "agent", and accordingly, need not be registered as a requirement for their employment. They are NOT, however, excluded in all circumstances simply because they are considered clerical or administrative. If they participate in functions that are securities related, they WILL be required to be registered employees. Further, providing a quote as requested by a client would NOT qualify as acting as an "agent" and accordingly, would NOT require their registration in order for them to continue performing their job. Also, if the company that employs them were to pay out a year-end annual bonus based on the company's OVERALL profits and performance, they WOULD be allowed to receive that bonus.

65. D: An employee asking a client over the phone if he would like to receive general information regarding the firm's services would NOT require registration as an agent in that there is no attempt to transact securities. However, an employee prequalifying clients for specific firm services; an employee making recommendations over the phone to clients regarding increasing profits within their stock portfolio; and a summer intern being paid for each client with whom she makes contact regarding potential activity in his portfolio do all require registration as an agent in that each involve actions that at least attempt effecting a securities transaction with a client.

66. D: The employee of an issuer will NOT be considered an agent when participating in transactions that are exempt from registration. Transactions with financial institutions, those between an issuer and underwriter, or private placements, are all exempt transactions and therefore would be NOT provide for the issuer's employee to be considered an agent. However, if the employee of the issuer received commissions, they would be considered an agent.

67. B: Per the Uniform Securities Act, debentures and collateral trust certificates are both considered to be "securities", and accordingly, would be covered by the provisions of the act. Fixed annuity contracts and commodities such as grains would NOT be considered "securities" are therefore NOT subject to the provisions of the act.

68. A: When considering the Uniform Securities Act, all nonexempt securities must be registered in order to be sold. Further, exempt securities need not be registered to be sold, and accordingly, the sale of currencies does NOT require registration.

69. C: A secondary transaction is one in which the resulting proceeds of the sale do NOT go to the entity that originally brought the securities to the market. Instead, the proceeds go to the investor offering the shares for sale now. Accordingly, this type of transaction is also known as a non-issuer transaction. An issuer transaction involves the proceeds of the sale going to the issuer of those securities.

70. B: An investor making the request for issuer-only transactions would participate in initial public offerings (IPO's), primary offerings, and subsequent public offerings (SPOs). Secondary transactions would NOT be appropriate for this investor in that they are considered to be nonissuer transactions, and transacted between individual investors, not between the issuer and the investing public.

71. D: An Administrator's order will not become final until all the necessary notices to all of the involved parties are given, and an opportunity for a hearing is provided. Beyond that there must be an effort made to seek out the facts of the situation, provide written documentation to support the findings, and then formulate conclusions that are based in law.

72. A: For an issuer registration application, a state Administrator in California would normally require the issuer to provide the amount of securities to be offered in the state of California, a list of any additional states in which the securities will be offered, and notice of any adverse judgment(s) by the SEC associated with the offering. The amounts of securities to be offered in any additional states is NOT something that would be required by the state Administrator when filing a registration statement.

73. B: A broker/dealer's net capital requirement is defined as his liquidated net worth. It may be set by his state Administrator, and if met, no posting of bonds beyond those requirements will be necessary. If a broker/dealer meets the net capital requirement set for him by the SEC, he they will NOT be required to satisfy a higher capital requirement set by his state Administrator. In fact, in matters such as this one, the state Administrator hands over primary authority to the SEC, leaving the net capital requirement set by the SEC as the only requirement the broker/dealer has the responsibility to meet.

74. A: A summary order can postpone or suspend an individual's securities registration, postpone or suspend a security's registration, or deny or revoke an exemption related to a security or transaction. Accordingly, this type of order is associated with the registration of BOTH individuals and securities. A stop order is an action that only applies to securities, and a cease-and-desist order can only apply to registered individuals.

75. B: For a state-covered adviser, the requirements regarding disclosing these legal actions to a prospective client depend on when they occurred. Here, only actions within the last 10 years must be disclosed, so the older action, not both must be disclosed. For a federally-covered adviser, disclosures of this nature are made via a brochure that is provided to the client. Therefore, the "48-hour rule" does NOT apply.

76. A: The Securities Act of 1933 requires the issuer of an offering to provide accurate disclosures regarding itself and the offering, requires that an investor have made available to him all material information regarding the offering he may require in determining its merits and impacting his decision to invest, and most importantly, made the way for providing criminal penalties for those committing fraud in the issuance of an offering of new securities.

77. C: PASSIVE management style involves primarily putting together a portfolio of securities that will be able to mimic the activity and performance of a market index. Minimal turnover of securities within the portfolio and keeping transaction costs low are also characteristics of this type of asset management. An ACTIVE management style attempts to achieve higher returns by trading in and out of stocks, utilizes market timing to outperform a market index, and focuses on securities in fewer market sectors to achieve higher returns.

78. D: Opportunity cost is the return given up on other investments when you choose a specific investment. Opportunity cost cannot be reduced or avoided as every decision requires one to choose one option over others and each option forgone has its own benefits one gives up by not choosing it. Liquidity risk is the risk that an investor won't be able to liquidate or receive cash for their investment in a timely manner.

79. A: An individual who has just graduated with an MBA in finance and publishes an online newsletter offering general comments on where she sees the future direction of the overall market going would NOT be considered to be an investment adviser nor would she be subject to regulation. Although providing analysis, she is making general comments, she is not in the business of doing so, and is not being compensated for her analysis. The financial analyst, entertainment representative, and broker/dealer representative ALL would be considered to be investment advisers and subject to regulation due to providing specific market advice, making it their business to do so, and being compensated (even indirectly) for their services.

80. C: Advisory services need NOT be charged separately from other broker/dealer services. Adviser compensation may include commissions, and other types of fees. "Special compensation" for advisory services go beyond the fees paid for typical broker/dealer services. Advisory services need not be paid for directly by the recipient of the advice, and may be paid for by a third party.

81. A: Section 28(e)'s safe harbor provision of the Securities Exchange Act of 1934 specifies that the research provided can be EITHER proprietary (created and distributed by the broker/dealer), OR created by a third party and then passed through to the broker/dealer for distribution to his or her clients. Research can also be provided via publications and can include portfolio analysis and strategy. Brokerage services can include transaction settlements.

82. B: An investment adviser receiving payment to cover travel expenses that are incurred while attending a research seminar would NOT be covered under 28(e) of the Securities Exchange Act of 1934 due to being a benefit to the adviser that is not research related. Soft dollar arrangements involve research related products or services that are provided to an investment adviser by a broker/dealer in exchange for the adviser "directing" client transactions to the broker/dealer. Examples of items that are covered under 28(e) are an investment adviser attending a research conference put on by the broker/dealer firm, receiving analytical software, and receiving research reports analyzing the current and future performance of one specific company.

83. C: With regard to the NASAA model rule, an adviser should provide safeguards to his clients related to the direct fee deduction arrangement he has made with his clients' accounts. First is a notice of fees being deducted, including the amount to be deducted. Second is a written authorization allowing the deduction of advisory fees. Third, involves providing notice to the Administrator of all of the safeguards the adviser intends to provide.

84. A: Discretionary trading authority must be accomplished in writing and must provide specifically for giving authority to trade. The business manager would NOT have discretionary trading authority given that executing a document to that effect does not transfer authority until the individual actually takes receipt of the written authorization. An attorney who simply has a power of attorney would NOT qualify as having discretionary trading authority. The business partner who has taken receipt of the document granting him trading authorization, and the attorney given written authority to trade would BOTH qualify as having discretionary trading authority.

85. B: A fiduciary MAY assign a portion of the fiduciary responsibilities to a third party if he does not feel qualified to fulfill that role in the best interest of that individual. A fiduciary may be either a receiver in a bankruptcy or a trustee for a trust account, and a fiduciary operating in a legal list state would be limited in the securities he could purchase for the account.

86. C: Per ERISA provisions, a fiduciary must act as prudent as the average expert, and his primary efforts should NOT be in maximizing profits while assuming larger risk, but instead, he should be minimizing losses while minimizing risk.

87. C: When an individual opens an account, it is required that she provide a variety of suitability information to include net worth, tax status, risk tolerance, and investment objectives. Without this information, the broker/dealer or investment adviser cannot adequately provide the most appropriate investment advice to this potential client. Accordingly, if the account is with a broker/dealer, the account may be opened but only to transact unsolicited orders initiated by the client given that the broker/dealer's role is to make recommendations AND execute transactions. Without the applicable client information, recommendations cannot be made. If the account is with an investment adviser, it must be refused until the suitability information is provided by the individual. The investment adviser's role is to give advice and without the appropriate suitability information recommendations cannot be made, orders cannot be accepted, and the account cannot be opened.

88. A: Per the Uniform Securities Act, a securities professional may only lend money or securities to or from a client if that client is either a broker/dealer, or a financial institution that makes it his business to participate in such lending services. Here, a security professional borrowing cash from his client, Union Bank, is deemed allowable due to this client being a financial institution who in the normal course of business loans funds to the public. The security professional either borrowing cash from his client's account, or lending cash to his client, are both unallowable per the Uniform Securities Act given that the client in both cases is NOT a broker/dealer or financial institution.

89. B: A violation of insider trading requires that an actual transaction take place that is based in the receipt of a company's material, nonpublic information. A violation can be committed by almost anyone who is in possession of a company's nonpublic information and can be punishable by the payment of treble damages. Treble damages allow for the violator to potentially be fined up to three times either the gains gotten or losses avoided by acting on the inside information.

90. B: Establishing an account that is fictitious for the purpose of executing transactions that are prohibited in nature is NOT considered to be a permissible practice. A broker/dealer authorizing his agent in writing to execute a transaction that will then not be recorded on the regular books and records of the firm is permissible due to the prior authorization that was given. An agent sharing in the profits of his client's accounts is considered permissible due to the prior written authorization received from the client and the agent's broker/dealer to do so. Per the Uniform Securities Act, a securities professional may only lend money or securities to or from a client if that client is either a broker/dealer, or a financial institution that makes it his business to participate in such lending services. Here, a security professional borrowing cash from his client, Union Bank, is deemed allowable due to this client being a financial institution who in the normal course of business loans funds to the public.

91. B: An individual account is an account where one beneficial non-business owner has singular control over the investments in the account, as well as the ability to request distributions from the account. A sole proprietorship is similar to an individual account except for being an individual business owner. Joint tenants with right of survivorship and tenants in common are both joint accounts, owned by two or more adults.

92. C: A general partner is required to maintain a financial interest in the partnership of at least 1%, NOT 3%. A general partner is responsible for buying and selling property for the partnership, and the decisions made by the general partner will be fully binding to the partnership.

93. A: A limited partner in a limited partnership will primarily act as a passive investor, taking no personal responsibility for any indebtedness that the partnership experiences and taking receipt of the partnerships gains and cash distributions. He will NOT assume responsibility for even limited operational functions of the partnership.

94. A: The business structures that will provide for the owner limited liability and a pass-through of both profits and losses are the limited liability company (LLC), limited partnership, and S corporation. A C corporation does provide the owner with limited liability but no pass-through of profits and losses given that the company is viewed as a separate entity from the owners.

95. D: An adviser must always assess a new client's personal and financial profile in order to establish a suitable investment plan. In order to do that, many different aspects of the client's profile must be looked into. The adviser should request the client's retirement account information, security holdings as well as his or her value totals, and credit card debt totals.

96. D: The non-financial items that would be relevant for an adviser to request in order to complete a client's profile would be the historical stability of the client's employment, the future educational needs for the client or his family, and the individual's investment knowledge and experience. His employment stability speaks to the potential future reliability of his employment status and thus, income; future educational plans indicate predictably large income needs in the future; and his investment knowledge allows the adviser insight into what types of investments he may be comfortable with and/or the degree to which the advisor needs to provide investment education beyond advisement.

97. B: In an effort to understand a new client's risk tolerance an investment adviser should discuss with the client, his ability to tolerate a variety of market fluctuations, and the desired time horizon for his investment portfolio, long-term or short. Although the number of dependents he has and current employment status could be useful in making inferences about his current financial situation, they would not be useful in gaining any direct knowledge regarding his risk tolerance.

98. C: An individual's incidents of ownership in a life insurance policy can be evidenced by his or her ability to assign ownership of the policy, modify the policy in any way, designate a beneficiary, and borrow money from the cash value of the policy.

99. B: Modern Portfolio Theory primarily focuses on the concept of controlling portfolio risk and in doing that examines the relationship that exists between risk and reward in the overall portfolio rather than for each of the independent securities. It theoretically stands for the idea that risk can be diversified away by building a certain type of portfolio, specifically one that has securities with returns that are not correlated. It further promotes diversification as a reducer of risk and the main contributing factor in causing an increase in returns. It analyzes the relationships that exist BETWEEN the investments in a portfolio rather than each of the individual stocks, and also seeks to prove that a lower, NOT higher amount of portfolio volatility, will produce better returns.

100. D: An efficient portfolio is one that either provides high return for a balanced amount of risk, or low risk with a balanced amount of return provided. The efficient frontier is a collection of those efficient portfolios all plotted on a curve and accordingly, is used as an aid in constructing the most efficient portfolio. Once established it provides a reference point for evaluating portfolios, below which lie the inefficient, lower return/higher risk portfolios. It is NOT, however, simply made up of portfolios that generally provide the most return, but instead those that provide the most return given a balanced amount of risk relative to that level of return. It does NOT seek high returns without consideration to the degree of risk to be taken.

101. C: The semi-strong form of the Efficient Market Hypothesis (EMH) is based on the idea that current security pricing already reflects all public information that is available. Accordingly, fundamental analysis would not be a tool that would produce better than average returns. Strong-form EMH seeks to support the idea that current security prices already reflect all public AND private information. Weak-form EMH states that security prices already reflect all market data currently available making it meaningless to analyze historical security or market data, and thus making the benefit of technical analysis negligible.

102. C: Valuation ratios help investors analyze a company's performance by providing a snapshot glimpse of related data compared to each other. For example, the price-to-earnings ratio compares the share price to the company's earnings per share, and the price-to-book ratio compares share price to the company's book value (company value based on assets vs liabilities). While helpful, one by itself does not provide enough information to warrant purchasing a security. Current and quick ratios are financial ratios, not valuation ratios. Financial ratios are a comparison of 2 specific numbers taken from financial statements.

103. B: Strategic asset allocation would best suit this client in that the focus there is on creating a portfolio with not only the best mix of assets, but also the best proportion of assets within the portfolio. The manager there would regularly examine the portfolio in an effort to identify areas in need of rebalance in order to maintain the optimal proportion of asset types. With tactical asset allocation attention is given to responding to a changing market. Short-term portfolio adjustments are made to the asset class mix in response to market movements.

104. A: Initial portfolio: $80,000

55% equity, $44,000 / 45% debt, $36,000

Portfolio increased to: $105,000, equity portion increasing to $69,000

Current portfolio: $105,000

66% equity, $69,000 / 34% debt, $36,000

TARGET portfolio after rebalancing: $105,000

55% equity, $58,000 / 45% debt, $47,000

Equities: $69,000 - $58,000 = $11,000

In order to rebalance the portfolio the action to be taken is to:

SELL $11,000 in equities and BUY $11,000 in debt.

105. C: original total asset value of the portfolio: $150,000

stocks $110,000 / remaining $40,000 invested in debt

stock portion increases to a value of $135,000

$$\$135,000 - \$110,000 = \$25,000 \text{ total stock increase}$$

In order to reach this client's constant dollar goal of $110,000 in stocks he must sell off the $25,000 in stock gains and reinvest that amount in debt.

$$\$40,000 \text{ debt} + \$25,000 \text{ invested gains} = \$65,000 \text{ total debt}$$

adjusted total asset value of the portfolio: $175,000

stocks $110,000 / remaining $65,000 now invested in debt

106. A: An active portfolio management style requires a manager with consistently successful market timing abilities, and is similar to tactical asset allocation. Active management seeks to OUTPERFORM market indexes, whereas a passive management style seeks to mimic a market index. It further involves buying and selling in and out of individual stocks in order to meet investment goals without any focus placed on minimizing transaction costs or turnover.

107. C: An investment manager with a growth style of management would seek out stocks that are at their 52-week price high. He or she is essentially looking for stocks that have already experienced great growth relative to other comparable stocks, and those that will experience further growth going forward. Conversely, stocks that show great future growth potential based solely on the information found in the company financial statements, are priced low relative to the company's earnings, and have a low P/E ratio are considered to be value stocks.

108. D: Portfolio diversification involves stocks being chosen because of their negative correlation to each other in order to maximize long-term gains. Further true is that this diversified group of stocks will contribute to reducing unsystematic risk in the portfolio in part by causing business risk to decrease. An increase in returns will follow accordingly.

109. B: Dollar cost averaging involves investing consistent amounts of money, NOT varying, and at regular intervals, in an effort to achieve purchasing a security over time at an average cost that is lower than its average price over the same period. It has the investor increasing the number of shares purchased when prices are low, and decreasing the number purchased when prices are high, and ultimately reduces the timing risk of purchasing shares at a high.

110. C: Progressive taxes are more demanding of individuals with high incomes in that as an individual's income increases, so does his respective tax rate. Regressive taxes are imposed at the same rate for all income levels and therefore, consume a larger percentage of income for those with lower incomes. Additionally, a payroll tax is a type of regressive tax, NOT progressive. Flat taxes impose the same percentage on each taxpayer across income levels.

111. A: A marginal tax rate is the rate imposed on an individual's income at its highest level. Here, the rate for income earned between \$155,000 and \$310,000 is 27%. Accordingly, this individual having reported earnings of \$301,750 would be said to have a marginal tax rate of 27%.

112. D:

$$\text{stock sale proceeds} - \text{cost to purchase stock} = \text{potential capital gain}$$

$$\begin{aligned}\text{total capital gain} &= [(120 \times \$35) + (210 \times \$22.50)] - [(120 \times \$24) + (210 \times \$21)] \\ &= (\$4{,}200 + \$4{,}725) - (\$2{,}880 + \$4{,}410) \\ &= \$8{,}925 - \$7{,}290 \\ &= \$1{,}635 \text{ total capital gain}\end{aligned}$$

113. B:

$$\begin{aligned}\text{adjusted gross estate (AGE)} &= \text{gross estate} - (\text{funeral expenses} + \text{debts}) \\ &= \$12{,}755{,}000 - (\$32{,}551 + \$4{,}887 + \$1{,}660{,}233) \\ &= \$12{,}755{,}000 - \$1{,}697{,}671 \\ &= \$11{,}057{,}329\end{aligned}$$

114. C: Per the IRS, pension income would NOT qualify as compensation for the purposes of this client contributing to a traditional individual retirement account (IRA). Self-employment income, alimony, and monetary tips WOULD all qualify as compensation and would be appropriate for this client to use as contributions into an IRA.

115. D: Roth individual retirement accounts (IRAs) provide for contributions that are NOT tax-deductible, and withdrawal of contributions can be done tax-free. The maximum limit on contributions for individuals is \$6,500 per year (as of 2023), NOT \$8,000, and distributions from the account are NOT required to begin at 72 years old.

116. A: Of these choices, an eligible employee considering a variety of investment vehicles for his or her 403(b) plan could choose annuities or money market mutual funds. Commercial paper and life insurance policies are NOT allowable for his plan.

117. B: The Uniform Prudent Investor Act (UPIA) provided for many adjustments to the Employment Retirement Income Security Act of 1974 (ERISA). They include first that the prudence standard is not simply applied to choices regarding individual investments, but instead to investments as they are part of an overall total portfolio. Second, they include the provision that all restrictions be lifted regarding the types of investments that were allowable for trustees to invest in, and third, that a fiduciary's primary concern must be with balancing risk versus return. The UPIA enabled greater diversification in investment portfolios.

118. B: The Employment Retirement Income Security Act of 1974 states that there must be a specified time by which employees are entitled to receive their retirement benefits. The plan must be provided to employees in writing with annual updates provided, and in order to ensure fairness, employee benefits and contributions must be determined impartially per a formula method. However, the eligibility portion of the Act states that it is NOT enough that an employee simply be

21 or older: he must also have been employed there for at least one year, AND worked at least 1,000 hours in that year.

119. C: Per ERISA guidelines, fiduciaries must seek to minimize plan and investment expenses, must not proceed with investment decisions based on the amount of transaction costs involved, and must employ diversification in order to minimize large losses. They are NOT, however, held to the "prudent person" standard, and are instead held to the "prudent expert rule".

120. A: Coverdell ESAs allow for multiple contributions to be made to one account but not in excess of $2,000 per child per year. They do NOT allow for contributions to be tax-deductible, earnings ARE tax-deferred, and distributions are tax-free, but ONLY if used for educational expenses AND if taken before the age of 30.

121. C: Advertisements containing references to the performance of investment adviser recommendations may not be limited to successful recommendations, they MUST accurately reflect those resulting in losses as well as those resulting in gains. Advertisements are messages directed to more than one person and may not include testimonials of any kind. US advertising limitations apply across all mediums and are not limited to any particular one unless specifically written as such.

122. A: A college savings plan will have no residency requirement, no age limits in that it's available to both children and adults, and no state guarantee. It will NOT have a limited enrollment period, and instead will have enrollment available all year long.

123. D: For the purposes of rolling over the unused portion of his 529 plan, this individual could consider his stepbrother's spouse, his foster child, and his first cousin as immediate family but not his stepbrother's father. Ancestors of step-siblings do not count as family members for these purposes.

124. C: Limit orders involve a customer setting specific limits for either a buy or sell price. Given that this type of order will only be executed at the specific price or better, there will be the chance that the order will not reach the limit order price and accordingly won't be executed. Market orders are always guaranteed to be executed at the best price available. Stop orders/stop loss orders become market orders once the stock reaches a certain price. At that point, being a market order, the order will also be guaranteed to be executed.

125. B: Security prices are established through negotiation in the OTC market. Government and municipal bonds trade there also. The NYSE trades listed securities and unlike the OTC market which is regulated by FINRA, it is regulated by the NYSE.

126. C: The stated quote for stock PLS with a bid price of $21.00 and ask price of $21.75 is "21 to .75".

127. B: Inflation adjusted returns are called real rates of return. Net present value is the difference between the present value of an investment and its cost. The expected return is merely an estimate of an investment's return, and the internal rate of return is the discount rate that will make an investment's future value equal it's present.

128. A: expected return = (probability % of security #1 × possible return of #1) + (probability % of security #2 × possible return of #2) + (probability % of security #3 + possible return of #3)

$$(.37 \times 9\%) + (.24 \times 17\%) + (.55 \times 12\%) =$$

$$\mathbf{3.33\% + 4.08\% + 6.6\% = 14.01\%}$$

129. C: An investor seeking a specific rate of return on an investment would do BEST to utilize an internal rate of return (IRR) calculation. If the IRR is greater than his required rate of return, the investment will be considered acceptable for his purposes. Calculating the expected return and net present value will give him good insight regarding the investment but not as specific as the IRR. The real return is a calculation used to adjust returns for inflation.

130. D: A bond with a YTM less than its YTC trades at a discount, a bond with a YTC greater than its CY trades at a discount, and a bond with a YTM less than its CY trades at a premium.

How to Overcome Test Anxiety

Just the thought of taking a test is enough to make most people a little nervous. A test is an important event that can have a long-term impact on your future, so it's important to take it seriously and it's natural to feel anxious about performing well. But just because anxiety is normal, that doesn't mean that it's helpful in test taking, or that you should simply accept it as part of your life. Anxiety can have a variety of effects. These effects can be mild, like making you feel slightly nervous, or severe, like blocking your ability to focus or remember even a simple detail.

If you experience test anxiety—whether severe or mild—it's important to know how to beat it. To discover this, first you need to understand what causes test anxiety.

Causes of Test Anxiety

While we often think of anxiety as an uncontrollable emotional state, it can actually be caused by simple, practical things. One of the most common causes of test anxiety is that a person does not feel adequately prepared for their test. This feeling can be the result of many different issues such as poor study habits or lack of organization, but the most common culprit is time management. Starting to study too late, failing to organize your study time to cover all of the material, or being distracted while you study will mean that you're not well prepared for the test. This may lead to cramming the night before, which will cause you to be physically and mentally exhausted for the test. Poor time management also contributes to feelings of stress, fear, and hopelessness as you realize you are not well prepared but don't know what to do about it.

Other times, test anxiety is not related to your preparation for the test but comes from unresolved fear. This may be a past failure on a test, or poor performance on tests in general. It may come from comparing yourself to others who seem to be performing better or from the stress of living up to expectations. Anxiety may be driven by fears of the future—how failure on this test would affect your educational and career goals. These fears are often completely irrational, but they can still negatively impact your test performance.

Review Video: 3 Reasons You Have Test Anxiety
Visit mometrix.com/academy and enter code: 428468

Elements of Test Anxiety

As mentioned earlier, test anxiety is considered to be an emotional state, but it has physical and mental components as well. Sometimes you may not even realize that you are suffering from test anxiety until you notice the physical symptoms. These can include trembling hands, rapid heartbeat, sweating, nausea, and tense muscles. Extreme anxiety may lead to fainting or vomiting. Obviously, any of these symptoms can have a negative impact on testing. It is important to recognize them as soon as they begin to occur so that you can address the problem before it damages your performance.

Review Video: 3 Ways to Tell You Have Test Anxiety
Visit mometrix.com/academy and enter code: 927847

The mental components of test anxiety include trouble focusing and inability to remember learned information. During a test, your mind is on high alert, which can help you recall information and stay focused for an extended period of time. However, anxiety interferes with your mind's natural processes, causing you to blank out, even on the questions you know well. The strain of testing during anxiety makes it difficult to stay focused, especially on a test that may take several hours. Extreme anxiety can take a huge mental toll, making it difficult not only to recall test information but even to understand the test questions or pull your thoughts together.

Review Video: How Test Anxiety Affects Memory
Visit mometrix.com/academy and enter code: 609003

Effects of Test Anxiety

Test anxiety is like a disease—if left untreated, it will get progressively worse. Anxiety leads to poor performance, and this reinforces the feelings of fear and failure, which in turn lead to poor performances on subsequent tests. It can grow from a mild nervousness to a crippling condition. If allowed to progress, test anxiety can have a big impact on your schooling, and consequently on your future.

Test anxiety can spread to other parts of your life. Anxiety on tests can become anxiety in any stressful situation, and blanking on a test can turn into panicking in a job situation. But fortunately, you don't have to let anxiety rule your testing and determine your grades. There are a number of relatively simple steps you can take to move past anxiety and function normally on a test and in the rest of life.

Review Video: How Test Anxiety Impacts Your Grades
Visit mometrix.com/academy and enter code: 939819

Physical Steps for Beating Test Anxiety

While test anxiety is a serious problem, the good news is that it can be overcome. It doesn't have to control your ability to think and remember information. While it may take time, you can begin taking steps today to beat anxiety.

Just as your first hint that you may be struggling with anxiety comes from the physical symptoms, the first step to treating it is also physical. Rest is crucial for having a clear, strong mind. If you are tired, it is much easier to give in to anxiety. But if you establish good sleep habits, your body and mind will be ready to perform optimally, without the strain of exhaustion. Additionally, sleeping well helps you to retain information better, so you're more likely to recall the answers when you see the test questions.

Getting good sleep means more than going to bed on time. It's important to allow your brain time to relax. Take study breaks from time to time so it doesn't get overworked, and don't study right before bed. Take time to rest your mind before trying to rest your body, or you may find it difficult to fall asleep.

Review Video: The Importance of Sleep for Your Brain
Visit mometrix.com/academy and enter code: 319338

Along with sleep, other aspects of physical health are important in preparing for a test. Good nutrition is vital for good brain function. Sugary foods and drinks may give a burst of energy but this burst is followed by a crash, both physically and emotionally. Instead, fuel your body with protein and vitamin-rich foods.

Also, drink plenty of water. Dehydration can lead to headaches and exhaustion, especially if your brain is already under stress from the rigors of the test. Particularly if your test is a long one, drink water during the breaks. And if possible, take an energy-boosting snack to eat between sections.

Review Video: How Diet Can Affect your Mood
Visit mometrix.com/academy and enter code: 624317

Along with sleep and diet, a third important part of physical health is exercise. Maintaining a steady workout schedule is helpful, but even taking 5-minute study breaks to walk can help get your blood pumping faster and clear your head. Exercise also releases endorphins, which contribute to a positive feeling and can help combat test anxiety.

When you nurture your physical health, you are also contributing to your mental health. If your body is healthy, your mind is much more likely to be healthy as well. So take time to rest, nourish your body with healthy food and water, and get moving as much as possible. Taking these physical steps will make you stronger and more able to take the mental steps necessary to overcome test anxiety.

Mental Steps for Beating Test Anxiety

Working on the mental side of test anxiety can be more challenging, but as with the physical side, there are clear steps you can take to overcome it. As mentioned earlier, test anxiety often stems from lack of preparation, so the obvious solution is to prepare for the test. Effective studying may be the most important weapon you have for beating test anxiety, but you can and should employ several other mental tools to combat fear.

First, boost your confidence by reminding yourself of past success—tests or projects that you aced. If you're putting as much effort into preparing for this test as you did for those, there's no reason you should expect to fail here. Work hard to prepare; then trust your preparation.

Second, surround yourself with encouraging people. It can be helpful to find a study group, but be sure that the people you're around will encourage a positive attitude. If you spend time with others who are anxious or cynical, this will only contribute to your own anxiety. Look for others who are motivated to study hard from a desire to succeed, not from a fear of failure.

Third, reward yourself. A test is physically and mentally tiring, even without anxiety, and it can be helpful to have something to look forward to. Plan an activity following the test, regardless of the outcome, such as going to a movie or getting ice cream.

When you are taking the test, if you find yourself beginning to feel anxious, remind yourself that you know the material. Visualize successfully completing the test. Then take a few deep, relaxing breaths and return to it. Work through the questions carefully but with confidence, knowing that you are capable of succeeding.

Developing a healthy mental approach to test taking will also aid in other areas of life. Test anxiety affects more than just the actual test—it can be damaging to your mental health and even contribute to depression. It's important to beat test anxiety before it becomes a problem for more than testing.

Review Video: Test Anxiety and Depression
Visit mometrix.com/academy and enter code: 904704

Study Strategy

Being prepared for the test is necessary to combat anxiety, but what does being prepared look like? You may study for hours on end and still not feel prepared. What you need is a strategy for test prep. The next few pages outline our recommended steps to help you plan out and conquer the challenge of preparation.

Step 1: Scope Out the Test

Learn everything you can about the format (multiple choice, essay, etc.) and what will be on the test. Gather any study materials, course outlines, or sample exams that may be available. Not only will this help you to prepare, but knowing what to expect can help to alleviate test anxiety.

Step 2: Map Out the Material

Look through the textbook or study guide and make note of how many chapters or sections it has. Then divide these over the time you have. For example, if a book has 15 chapters and you have five days to study, you need to cover three chapters each day. Even better, if you have the time, leave an extra day at the end for overall review after you have gone through the material in depth.

If time is limited, you may need to prioritize the material. Look through it and make note of which sections you think you already have a good grasp on, and which need review. While you are studying, skim quickly through the familiar sections and take more time on the challenging parts. Write out your plan so you don't get lost as you go. Having a written plan also helps you feel more in control of the study, so anxiety is less likely to arise from feeling overwhelmed at the amount to cover.

Step 3: Gather Your Tools

Decide what study method works best for you. Do you prefer to highlight in the book as you study and then go back over the highlighted portions? Or do you type out notes of the important information? Or is it helpful to make flashcards that you can carry with you? Assemble the pens, index cards, highlighters, post-it notes, and any other materials you may need so you won't be distracted by getting up to find things while you study.

If you're having a hard time retaining the information or organizing your notes, experiment with different methods. For example, try color-coding by subject with colored pens, highlighters, or post-it notes. If you learn better by hearing, try recording yourself reading your notes so you can listen while in the car, working out, or simply sitting at your desk. Ask a friend to quiz you from your flashcards, or try teaching someone the material to solidify it in your mind.

Step 4: Create Your Environment

It's important to avoid distractions while you study. This includes both the obvious distractions like visitors and the subtle distractions like an uncomfortable chair (or a too-comfortable couch that makes you want to fall asleep). Set up the best study environment possible: good lighting and a comfortable work area. If background music helps you focus, you may want to turn it on, but otherwise keep the room quiet. If you are using a computer to take notes, be sure you don't have any other windows open, especially applications like social media, games, or anything else that could distract you. Silence your phone and turn off notifications. Be sure to keep water close by so you stay hydrated while you study (but avoid unhealthy drinks and snacks).

Also, take into account the best time of day to study. Are you freshest first thing in the morning? Try to set aside some time then to work through the material. Is your mind clearer in the afternoon or evening? Schedule your study session then. Another method is to study at the same time of day that you will take the test, so that your brain gets used to working on the material at that time and will be ready to focus at test time.

Step 5: Study!

Once you have done all the study preparation, it's time to settle into the actual studying. Sit down, take a few moments to settle your mind so you can focus, and begin to follow your study plan. Don't give in to distractions or let yourself procrastinate. This is your time to prepare so you'll be ready to fearlessly approach the test. Make the most of the time and stay focused.

Of course, you don't want to burn out. If you study too long you may find that you're not retaining the information very well. Take regular study breaks. For example, taking five minutes out of every hour to walk briskly, breathing deeply and swinging your arms, can help your mind stay fresh.

As you get to the end of each chapter or section, it's a good idea to do a quick review. Remind yourself of what you learned and work on any difficult parts. When you feel that you've mastered the material, move on to the next part. At the end of your study session, briefly skim through your notes again.

But while review is helpful, cramming last minute is NOT. If at all possible, work ahead so that you won't need to fit all your study into the last day. Cramming overloads your brain with more information than it can process and retain, and your tired mind may struggle to recall even previously learned information when it is overwhelmed with last-minute study. Also, the urgent nature of cramming and the stress placed on your brain contribute to anxiety. You'll be more likely to go to the test feeling unprepared and having trouble thinking clearly.

So don't cram, and don't stay up late before the test, even just to review your notes at a leisurely pace. Your brain needs rest more than it needs to go over the information again. In fact, plan to finish your studies by noon or early afternoon the day before the test. Give your brain the rest of the day to relax or focus on other things, and get a good night's sleep. Then you will be fresh for the test and better able to recall what you've studied.

Step 6: Take a Practice Test

Many courses offer sample tests, either online or in the study materials. This is an excellent resource to check whether you have mastered the material, as well as to prepare for the test format and environment.

Check the test format ahead of time: the number of questions, the type (multiple choice, free response, etc.), and the time limit. Then create a plan for working through them. For example, if you have 30 minutes to take a 60-question test, your limit is 30 seconds per question. Spend less time on the questions you know well so that you can take more time on the difficult ones.

If you have time to take several practice tests, take the first one open book, with no time limit. Work through the questions at your own pace and make sure you fully understand them. Gradually work up to taking a test under test conditions: sit at a desk with all study materials put away and set a timer. Pace yourself to make sure you finish the test with time to spare and go back to check your answers if you have time.

After each test, check your answers. On the questions you missed, be sure you understand why you missed them. Did you misread the question (tests can use tricky wording)? Did you forget the information? Or was it something you hadn't learned? Go back and study any shaky areas that the practice tests reveal.

Taking these tests not only helps with your grade, but also aids in combating test anxiety. If you're already used to the test conditions, you're less likely to worry about it, and working through tests until you're scoring well gives you a confidence boost. Go through the practice tests until you feel comfortable, and then you can go into the test knowing that you're ready for it.

Test Tips

On test day, you should be confident, knowing that you've prepared well and are ready to answer the questions. But aside from preparation, there are several test day strategies you can employ to maximize your performance.

First, as stated before, get a good night's sleep the night before the test (and for several nights before that, if possible). Go into the test with a fresh, alert mind rather than staying up late to study.

Try not to change too much about your normal routine on the day of the test. It's important to eat a nutritious breakfast, but if you normally don't eat breakfast at all, consider eating just a protein bar. If you're a coffee drinker, go ahead and have your normal coffee. Just make sure you time it so that the caffeine doesn't wear off right in the middle of your test. Avoid sugary beverages, and drink enough water to stay hydrated but not so much that you need a restroom break 10 minutes into the test. If your test isn't first thing in the morning, consider going for a walk or doing a light workout before the test to get your blood flowing.

Allow yourself enough time to get ready, and leave for the test with plenty of time to spare so you won't have the anxiety of scrambling to arrive in time. Another reason to be early is to select a good seat. It's helpful to sit away from doors and windows, which can be distracting. Find a good seat, get out your supplies, and settle your mind before the test begins.

When the test begins, start by going over the instructions carefully, even if you already know what to expect. Make sure you avoid any careless mistakes by following the directions.

Then begin working through the questions, pacing yourself as you've practiced. If you're not sure on an answer, don't spend too much time on it, and don't let it shake your confidence. Either skip it and come back later, or eliminate as many wrong answers as possible and guess among the remaining ones. Don't dwell on these questions as you continue—put them out of your mind and focus on what lies ahead.

Be sure to read all of the answer choices, even if you're sure the first one is the right answer. Sometimes you'll find a better one if you keep reading. But don't second-guess yourself if you do immediately know the answer. Your gut instinct is usually right. Don't let test anxiety rob you of the information you know.

If you have time at the end of the test (and if the test format allows), go back and review your answers. Be cautious about changing any, since your first instinct tends to be correct, but make sure you didn't misread any of the questions or accidentally mark the wrong answer choice. Look over any you skipped and make an educated guess.

At the end, leave the test feeling confident. You've done your best, so don't waste time worrying about your performance or wishing you could change anything. Instead, celebrate the successful completion of this test. And finally, use this test to learn how to deal with anxiety even better next time.

Review Video: 5 Tips to Beat Test Anxiety
Visit mometrix.com/academy and enter code: 570656

Important Qualification

Not all anxiety is created equal. If your test anxiety is causing major issues in your life beyond the classroom or testing center, or if you are experiencing troubling physical symptoms related to your anxiety, it may be a sign of a serious physiological or psychological condition. If this sounds like your situation, we strongly encourage you to seek professional help.

Thank You

We at Mometrix would like to extend our heartfelt thanks to you, our friend and patron, for allowing us to play a part in your journey. It is a privilege to serve people from all walks of life who are unified in their commitment to building the best future they can for themselves.

The preparation you devote to these important testing milestones may be the most valuable educational opportunity you have for making a real difference in your life. We encourage you to put your heart into it—that feeling of succeeding, overcoming, and yes, conquering will be well worth the hours you've invested.

We want to hear your story, your struggles and your successes, and if you see any opportunities for us to improve our materials so we can help others even more effectively in the future, please share that with us as well. **The team at Mometrix would be absolutely thrilled to hear from you!** So please, send us an email (support@mometrix.com) and let's stay in touch.

If you'd like some additional help, check out these other resources we offer for your exam:
http://MometrixFlashcards.com/Series65

Additional Bonus Material

Due to our efforts to try to keep this book to a manageable length, we've created a link that will give you access to all of your additional bonus material:

mometrix.com/bonus948/series65